PRISON CONDITIONS IN SOUTH AFRICA

Africa Watch
Prison Project

Human Rights Watch
New York • Washington • Los Angeles • London

Copyright © February 1994 by Human Rights Watch
All rights reserved.
Printed in the United States of America

Library of Congress Catalog Card No.: 93-81326
ISBN 1-56432-126-6

Africa Watch
Africa Watch is a nongovernmental organization established in 1988 to monitor and promote the observance of internationally recognized human rights in Africa. The chair is William Carmichael; the vice-chair is Alice Brown. Abdullahi An-Na'im is executive director; Janet Fleischman is the Washington Representative; Bronwen Manby, Karen Sorenson and Alex Vines are research associates; Kimberly Mazyck and Urmi Shah are Associates.

The Prison Project
The Prison Project, established in 1988, cuts across the five regional divisions of Human Rights Watch to focus on a single issue: prison conditions worldwide. The Prison Project has investigated conditions for sentenced prisoners, pre-trial detainees, and those held in police lockups. It examines prison conditions for all prisoners, not just political prisoners. The work of the Prison Project is guided by the Prison Advisory Committee, whose chair is Herman Schwartz. Other members are Nan Aron, Vivian Berger, Haywood Burns, Alejandro Garro, William Hellerstein, Edward Koren, Sheldon Krantz, The Honorable Morris Lasker, Benjamin Malcolm, Diane Orentlicher, Norman Rosenberg, David Rothman, and Clarence Sundram. The director of the Project is Joanna Weschler. Anthony Levintow is the associate.

For a catalog of publications, please call (212) 986-1980.

HUMAN RIGHTS WATCH

Human Rights Watch conducts regular, systematic investigations of human rights abuses in some seventy countries around the world. It addresses the human rights practices of governments of all political stripes, of all geopolitical alignments, and of all ethnic and religious persuasions. In internal wars it documents violations by both governments and rebel groups. Human Rights Watch defends freedom of thought and expression, due process and equal protection of the law; it documents and denounces murders, disappearances, torture, arbitrary imprisonment, exile, censorship and other abuses of internationally recognized human rights.

Human Rights Watch began in 1978 with the founding of its Helsinki division. Today, it includes five divisions covering Africa, the Americas, Asia, the Middle East, as well as the signatories of the Helsinki accords. It also includes four collaborative projects on Arms, Free Expression, Prisoners' Rights, and Women's Rights. It now maintains offices in New York, Washington, Los Angeles, London, Moscow, Belgrade, Zagreb and Hong Kong. Human Rights Watch is an independent, nongovernmental organization, supported by contributions from private individuals and foundations. It accepts no government funds, directly or indirectly.

The board includes Robert L. Bernstein, chair; Adrian W. DeWind, vice chair; Roland Algrant, Lisa Anderson, Peter D. Bell, Alice L. Brown, William Carmichael, Dorothy Cullman, Irene Diamond, Jonathan Fanton, Alan Finberg, Jack Greenberg, Alice H. Henkin, Stephen L. Kass, Marina Pinto Kaufman, Alexander MacGregor, Peter Osnos, Kathleen Peratis, Bruce Rabb, Orville Schell, Gary G. Sick, and Malcolm Smith.

The staff includes Kenneth Roth, executive director; Holly J. Burkhalter, Washington director; Gara LaMarche, associate director; Susan Osnos, press director; Ellen Lutz, California director; Jemera Rone, counsel; Richard Dicker, associate counsel; Michal Longfelder, development director; Rachel Weintraub, special events director; Allyson Collins, research associate; and Ham Fish, senior advisor.

The regional directors of Human Rights Watch are Abdullahi An-Na'im, Africa; Juan E. Méndez, Americas; Sidney Jones, Asia; Jeri Laber, Helsinki; and Andrew Whitley, Middle East. The project directors are Kenneth Anderson, Arms Project; Gara LaMarche, Free Expression Project; Joanna Weschler, Prison Project; and Dorothy Q. Thomas, Women's Rights Project.

Addresses for Human Rights Watch
485 Fifth Avenue
New York, NY 10017-6104
Tel: (212) 972-8400
Fax: (212) 972-0905
email: hrwatchnyc@igc.apc.org

1522 K Street, N.W., #910
Washington, DC 20005
Tel: (202) 371-6592
Fax: (202) 371-0124
email: hrwatchdc@igc.apc.org

10951 West Pico Blvd., #203
Los Angeles, CA 90064
Tel: (310) 475-3070
Fax: (310) 475-5613
email: hrwatchla@igc.apc.org

90 Borough High Street
London, UK SE1 1LL
Tel: (071) 378-8008
Fax: (071) 378-8029
email: hrwatchuk@gn.apc.org

CONTENTS

ACKNOWLEDGMENTS vii

INTRODUCTION ix

RECOMMENDATIONS xvi

I. RECENT CHANGES IN PRISON LEGISLATION 1
    SEGREGATION 1
    CENSORSHIP 2
    DISCIPLINARY MEASURES 4

II. PHYSICAL CIRCUMSTANCES 7
    OVERCROWDING 7
    TRANSFERS 10
    CELL CONDITIONS 11
    BEDDING AND CLOTHING 13
    FOOD 14
    MEDICAL CARE 15

III. DIFFERENT TREATMENT BASED ON RACE 17
    DISCRIMINATION AMONG PRISON STAFF 21

IV. THE "PRIVILEGE" SYSTEM 24

V. DISCIPLINARY MEASURES 28
    AUTHORIZED MEASURES 29
    UNAUTHORIZED MEASURES 37
    MISTREATMENT OF PARTICIPANTS IN NON-VIOLENT
        PROTESTS 41
    VIOLENCE IN THE AFTERMATH OF A PRISON RIOT 42

VI. GANGS AND VIOLENCE 43

VII. POLICE LOCKUPS 49
    PHYSICAL CONDITIONS 49
    VIOLENCE 50

VIII. CONTACTS WITH THE OUTSIDE 58
    VISITS 58
    CORRESPONDENCE 60
    USE OF THE TELEPHONE 60
    ACCESS TO NEWS 60

IX. WORK 63

X. ACTIVITIES 68
    RECREATION 68
    EDUCATION 69

XI. SPECIAL CATEGORIES OF PRISONERS 71
    WOMEN 71
    JUVENILES 73
    SECURITY PRISONERS 76
    JUDGMENT DEBTORS 78

RELEASE 79

PRISONS IN THE "INDEPENDENT" HOMELANDS 82

APPENDIX I 84

APPENDIX II 91

ACKNOWLEDGMENTS

This report is based on information gathered in the course of missions conducted in South Africa by Alice Brown, Vice-Chair of Africa Watch, and Joanna Weschler, Director of the Prison Project, in 1992; and by Bronwen Manby, a researcher with Africa Watch, in 1993. It was written by Weschler and Manby and edited by Cynthia Brown. Human Rights Watch wishes to thank the following individuals and organizations for their assistance in the course of our research: Prof. János Mihálik; Prof. Dirk Van Zyl Smit; Lawyers for Human Rights; Legal Resource Centre; POPCRU; NICRO; and Mojapelo & Co., Nelspruit.

INTRODUCTION

Prison conditions in South Africa have been directly affected by the political changes in the country since the beginning of 1990. Significant reforms of the system have been implemented, and conditions have improved in some respects. Nevertheless, at approximately 393 per 100,000, South Africa continues to have one of the highest prisoner-to-population ratios in the world, and many aspects of prison life remain depressingly unchanged from the years of official *apartheid*. In particular, South African prisons are places of extreme violence, where assaults on prisoners by guards or other prisoners are common and not infrequently fatal.

Africa Watch and the Prison Project of Human Rights Watch conducted an investigation of prison conditions in South Africa during 1992-93. During the course of two separate missions to the country, the following prison complexes were visited: Pretoria Central, Durban Westville, Robben Island, Pollsmoor, Rooigrond (Bophuthatswana), Umtata Central and Wellington (Transkei), Brandvlei, Kroonstad, Barberton and Modderbee; a total of over twenty individual prisons. We also conducted visits to police lockups in Cape Town, Verwoerdburg, Kensington, Khayelitsha and Soshanguve. In addition, we reviewed reported court cases dealing with prisoners' rights, and interviewed prison officials, former prisoners, prison reform advocates, prisoners' rights activists, and lawyers working on prison conditions.

South Africa's prison system was established in the nineteenth century, during the expansion of colonial rule from the Cape Peninsula to the modern boundaries of South Africa and beyond.[1] In 1910, the Union of South Africa was established, joining together the four provinces of Cape, Natal, Transvaal and the Orange Free State, and in 1911 a consolidated Prisons and Reformatories Act was passed. This legislation was replaced in 1959 with the Prisons Act, which — renamed the Correctional Services Act and amended many times — is still the basis of South African prison law today.

---

[1] For a history of the South African prison system, see Dirk Van Zyl Smit, *South African Prison Law and Practice*, (Durban: Butterworths, 1992), pp. 7-43.

The development of the prison system was closely linked to the progressive institutionalization of racial discrimination in South Africa, from the time that widely enforced "pass laws" were introduced for Africans in the 1870s, to the elaboration of an official theory and systematized practice of apartheid following the victory of the National Party in the election of 1948. The pass laws, which were introduced especially to regulate the labor force in the diamond and gold mines of Kimberley and the Witwatersrand, criminalized a vast number of otherwise law-abiding citizens. Sentenced to imprisonment, they were then used as convict labor by the mining companies, whose compounds for theoretically voluntarily employed migrant laborers were already scarcely better than prisons. At the same time, the increasing militarization of the South African state in its contacts with the majority population was extended to the prison system, where uniforms and military ranks were given to prison staff.

The Prisons Act "tightened up" the administration of prisons in several ways, in particular by removing the flimsy mechanisms of outside supervision that had existed and by restricting media coverage of prison conditions. Racial segregation, already codified under the 1911 act, was further reinforced. However, the new act was also framed with reference to the newly adopted United Nations Standard Minimum Rules for the Treatment of Prisoners, and in some respects an improvement on its predecessor, at least as written.

From the 1960s, ever-larger numbers of political prisoners were added to the South African prison population. Their writings and legal challenges to the authorities contributed to an international outcry at prison conditions. In 1964, the Red Cross was invited to visit South African prisons for the first time; in 1966 its report was published (despite the usual rules of strict confidentiality). Despite this focus on prisoners' rights, the South African authorities maintained, controversially, but with the acquiescence of the courts, that all but the most basic necessities for survival were privileges whose grant was in the sole discretion of the system. As opposition to apartheid outside the prison system became steadily more effective during the 1970s and 1980s, the response of the authorities also affected the situation inside prison walls. In 1985, the introduction of a state of emergency brought the detention without trial of large numbers of anti-apartheid activists, and increased restrictions on reporting, including reporting on prisons. Nevertheless, it became clear to at least a section of the ruling National Party, including State President

F.W. de Klerk, who replaced the hardline P.W. Botha in 1989, that the existing order could not be maintained against internal revolution and international isolation.

In February 1990, de Klerk announced the end of the state of emergency, the unbanning of the African National Congress (ANC) and other extraparliamentary opposition parties, and the release of Nelson Mandela and other famous political prisoners. A process of negotiation for the introduction of universal suffrage and democratic government in South Africa was begun. The prison system has been part of the general movement to reform government institutions that has accompanied the negotiations, and significant amendments to the Prisons Act have been introduced.

In 1990, apartheid in the prison system was formally abolished, with the repeal of the section requiring black and white prisoners to be housed separately. The Prisons Service was separated from the Department of Justice and renamed the Department of Correctional Services; the Prisons Act was renamed the Correctional Services Act in 1991. A new sentence of "correctional supervision" was also introduced, allowing the possibility of a reduction in the prison population and acknowledging the limited usefulness of custodial sentences. Further legislation drastically reduced the circumstances in which the death penalty might be imposed, all existing death sentences were reviewed and many commuted, and a moratorium on hangings was introduced. At the same time, restrictions on reporting of prison conditions were substantially removed, and outside supervision of the prison authorities increased, by the inclusion of non-prison staff on some of the committees regulating prison affairs. In 1993, further major amendments to the legislation curtailed the methods by which prisoners might be punished and introduced important new procedural safeguards.

One of the preconditions set by the ANC for the beginning of formal negotiations with the government was the release of all political prisoners; that is, of prisoners convicted under South Africa's draconian security legislation before it was reformed. In two "minutes" signed at Groote Schuur in May 1990 and at Pretoria in August 1990, the ANC and the government agreed on criteria for the definition of a political prisoner, and a review process was set out. The initial deadline under these procedures for the release of all political prisoners was April 30, 1991; although disagreements on classification — particularly as to whether individuals convicted of violent acts should be included in the definition — and bureaucratic delays meant that only a minority of those described as political by the ANC had been released at that date. Several hundred prisoners were nevertheless released by the end of the year, and in September 1992 further negotiations resulted in the release of 500 more prisoners; in total, approximately 1,600 security prisoners had been released by late 1993.[2]

During the same period, in response to overcrowding in the prison system, large numbers of common criminals were also granted early release; some 50,000 in 1991, and a further 7,500 announced in January 1993. Although welcomed in opposition circles, the release of security and other prisoners proved extremely controversial amongst white South Africans. Moreover, when combined with the publicity about release of political prisoners, it provoked an outburst of discontent in the prisons themselves amongst prisoners left out of the process. In 1991, hundreds of prisoners went on hunger strike demanding political status and early release; several prisons were hit by severe rioting. Hunger strikes by prisoners claiming political status continued over the following period, though they reduced in frequency and determination after the last large group of security prisoners was released by the government in late 1992. Even in 1993, however, there were widespread hunger strikes in prisons in January and February, organized by the South African Prisoners Organization for Human Rights (SAPOHR), a pressure group formed by ex-prisoners; and in May 1993, approximately twenty prisoners in Leeuwkop prison embarked on a strike in support of their claim to political status.

Reforms recently introduced also include the introduction of telephones for prisoner use (though on a limited basis); the curtailment of the use of straitjackets, and a much greater effort to segregate juvenile prisoners from adults.

Reform of the prison system is likely to continue. Furthermore, the interim constitution agreed at the negotiations for a transition to majority rule, which will come into effect in South Africa once multiracial

---

[2]The Human Rights Commission (HRC), an independent monitoring organization, calculated that forty-six prisoners fitting the criteria of the Groote Schuur and Pretoria minutes remained in the prison system at the end of October 1993. Of these, thirteen were already assessed to be political by the joint scrutiny committee; sixteen were under review by the committee, and the remainder appeared only on the HRC list.

elections take place, guarantees certain rights to prisoners and detainees. Although the exact effect of the bill of rights remains to be seen, explicit constitutionally-guaranteed rights will open up the possibility of substantive court supervision of the prison system (and of other aspects of government), hitherto restricted by the courts' endorsement of an extremely limited view of prisoners' rights.

Nevertheless, some aspects of the prison system are unlikely to change in the short term. South Africa has an extremely high rate of violent crime. Well over 20,000 people are murdered every year, roughly fifty for every 100,000 of the population (the figure for the United States is 17.2 per 100,000). Statistics for rape and other violent offenses are at similar levels. These numbers are unlikely to change until the economic and social crisis in the townships can be addressed — something that will take many years. In the meantime, there is little alternative to incarceration for violent offenders, the prisoner-to-population ratio will remain high, and overcrowding will remain the norm for most prisons. The high levels of violence observed in South African prisons are in part reflections of the violence of South African society in general, and will be difficult to eradicate without parallel progress outside prison walls. Equally, racism in the prison service, which remains a reality despite the legal reforms, reflects racism in the wider population.

Despite these problems, we believe that the prison system in South Africa could be substantially improved, even without major investments by the taxpayer. The recommendations made in this report suggest specific measures that would begin that process. Although some of these reforms could be instituted by the Department of Correctional Services on its own initiative, so far as possible reforms to the system should be carried out in consultation with prisoners' rights groups and other interested parties.

The investigation of prison conditions in South Africa carried out by Human Rights Watch has benefited from the recent reforms. Our representatives received unprecedented access to prisons and prisoners, with unlimited freedom to select the prisons visited. As a condition for this permission, Human Rights Watch agreed to give the Department of Correctional Services an opportunity to comment on a draft of the report before publication: the report as published takes into account many of the comments made by the Department. In the appendix, we also reproduce the Department's comments regarding some of our recommendations and provide our response to these comments.

This level of cooperation with an international monitoring organization would have been unthinkable a few years ago.[3] Nevertheless, it was clear to us that the spirit of reform shown by the decision to allow our prison visits to occur was not shared by all members of the Department of Correctional Services. While some prison officers welcomed our attention as an opportunity to press for further improvements, others were clearly resistant to any idea of modifying the violent culture of prison life; many prisoners expressed to us their fear of reprisals for talking to our representatives. Although the recent reforms should, in time, improve the conditions in which prisoners are held, we have included in our report references to the practices of the recent past, on the grounds that they remain relevant to describe the experiences of prisoners today. Even with complete commitment from senior prison management, it would be some years before many of the abuses we observed are likely to be eradicated. We hope that this contribution to the debate on penal reform in South Africa will encourage the continuation and extension of the reforms that have already been made.

The Prison Project of Human Rights Watch bases its assessment of prisons on international standards for the treatment of prisoners, especially the U.N. Standard Minimum Rules for the Treatment of Prisoners, adopted in 1955 by the First United Nations Congress on the Prevention of Crime and the Treatment of Offenders.[4] South Africa's Department of Correctional Services also accepts the U.N. Standard Minimum Rules as the basis of its practice. In addition, South Africa signed several human rights treaties during 1993, including the

---

[3] Access to all South African prisons was also given to the International Committee of the Red Cross (ICRC) in 1992. The ICRC had also been given permission to visit a limited number of security prisoners since the 1960s. However, ICRC reports (with the important exception of the report published in 1966) are confidential and available only to the authorities responsible for the prisons visited. Lawyers for Human Rights, a leading South African human rights organization, was also given access to several South African prisons during 1993.

[4] The complete text of the UN Standard Minimum Rules is attached as Appendix II.

Convention against Torture and Other Cruel Inhuman or Degrading Treatment or Punishment, indicating a new acceptance of international standards.[5]

---

[5] Although South Africa was among the countries present at the founding of the United Nations in 1945, it resisted for several decades all claims by the international community to have an interest in monitoring human rights within its borders, abstained from the resolution adopting the Universal Declaration of Human Rights (UDHR), and did not become a party to any of the major human rights treaties as they were drawn up. However, with the rolling- back of the apartheid legislation, this position was relaxed, and international scrutiny of human rights practices has increasingly been tolerated. As of the date of publication of this report, South Africa had not yet followed its signature with ratification of the Convention Against Torture. However, torture is illegal under international customary law, and the lack of ratification does not affect South Africa's general obligations to prevent its use. Moreover, the UDHR — which bans torture and other cruel inhuman or degrading treatment or punishment — is widely regarded as the authoritative interpretation of member states' human rights obligations under the U.N. Charter, to which South Africa has always remained a party.

RECOMMENDATIONS

The most primary recommendation that comes to emerge from our examination of South African prisons is that the South African Department of Correctional Services bring the reality of prison conditions into line with the newly enacted laws and regulations. Efforts should be made to bring the amending legislation into effect and to see that the newly eliminated disciplinary measures are indeed no longer used and that the other new provisions of the law are also adhered to. The racial integration of the prison system needs to be speeded up. Furthermore, conditions in the prisons that historically housed only black prisoners must be improved to match the standards that applied to institutions reserved for white inmates until the recent reforms.

In addition, we wish to make several specific recommendations, noted below. The majority of these relate to policy changes and do not require major financial investments. The one area where realizing our recommendations would require significant expenditure relates to education and job training. We consider this an investment that would pay off in the wider context of South African society because it would help prisoners to find meaningful employment upon their release and thus help prevent them from committing crimes and returning to prison in the future.

Benefits

o   The "privilege" system should be abolished. All inmates should be entitled to contact visits, allowed access to TV and press, given unlimited use of the library, permitted to write poetry and practice hobbies. Restrictions on these rights should be used only as disciplinary measures, for specified infractions and for limited periods of time.

o   Cases in which prisoners may be granted certain benefits at the discretion of prison officers should be reduced to a minimum. All such cases are opportunities for abuse.

Treatment of Juveniles

o   Juveniles should never be housed in adult institutions.

- Juveniles should never be transported together with adult prisoners.
- In institutions for juveniles, housing in separate age groups should always be a rule to avoid situations in which ten-year-olds might be housed with twenty-one-year-olds.

Abuse and Punishment

- All cases of alleged beatings of prisoners by guards or of collaboration by guards in the gang system should be thoroughly investigated, and staff members found guilty of applying unauthorized force should be disciplined.
- All statements by prisoners that they are in danger, as a result of gang activity or otherwise, should be taken with the utmost seriousness; inmates at risk should be removed from the cells in which they face that danger, to be placed in single cells whenever possible, if that is their request.
- There should be a thorough, independent investigation of the 1991 riot in Barberton prison, the six deaths and the subsequent alleged assaults against prisoners.
- The six-month limitation period applicable to court actions against the police or prison service for damages for assault should be raised to the usual three-year limitation period for civil actions.
- The provision making it a disciplinary infraction for prisoners to lodge a false complaint should be removed from the regulations.
- Restraints should never be applied as a disciplinary measure; when used to subdue a prisoner, they should only be applied as long as strictly necessary, and never for more than a few hours.
- Collective punishment should never be applied.
- Bans on reading should never be used as a disciplinary measure.

Access to Information

- All prisoners, including pre-trial detainees and unsentenced prisoners, should have unrestricted access to reading material.
- Every inmate should be issued a written copy in plain language of all rules applying to the prison where he or she is housed, including the content of orders of the Corrections Department

(also called Departmental Orders), as well as the relevant sections of the Correctional Services Act and Regulations. This guide should be issued in several South African languages, and each prison should have a system for notifying illiterate prisoners about the applicable rules of behavior.

Police Custody

o Prisoners, whether sentenced or pre-trial, should never be held in police lockups for more than 48 hours.
o Time spent in pre-trial detention should automatically count toward the sentence imposed if the accused is convicted.

Cells, Food and Exercise

o Cell space should be used evenly within each prison to avoid creating artificial overcrowding.
o All cells should be equipped with basic furniture such as beds, chairs, tables and cabinets or shelves for private belongings.
o Inmates should always be provided with three meals a day. Meal times should be spaced evenly during the day, to avoid excessively long periods between the last and the first meal of the day.
o All prisoners should have at a minimum, an hour of daily exercise.

Visits and Representation

o The provision making it an infraction to discuss prison conditions during visits should be removed from prison regulations.
o The restrictions on subjects that may be discussed or documents that may be handed over during meetings with a legal representative should be removed.
o Paralegals and trainee attorneys should be allowed equal access to prisoners as fully qualified attorneys or advocates.
o Efforts should be made to house prisoners as near to their area of habitual residence as possible, and all requests for transfers should be sympathetically assessed.

- For prisoners whose relatives must travel in order to visit, it should be possible to combine several shorter visits into a longer one or to conduct several visits in just a few days when visiting relatives are staying in the area where the prison is located.
- Telephone calls should not count as visits.

Training and Study

- Prisoners of all races and both sexes should have equal access to vocational training and to the most desirable prison jobs.
- Vocational training of a meaningful nature should be progressively expanded, ideally to be available to all prisoners, and especially to those deemed to be most likely to be involved in gang violence.
- Prisoners should be encouraged to study not only on the most basic level; efforts should be made to facilitate access to correspondence courses for all prisoners who are willing to study.

Warders' Performance

- Cases in which members and officers of the recently-legalized Police and Prison Civil Rights Union (POPCRU) have been disciplined, demoted or fired by the Department of Correctional Services should be investigated by an independent arbitrator, with power to order compensation and/or reinstatement if the action taken against them is found to be unwarranted.
- Military ranks and uniforms, and military-type discipline among prison warders, should be abolished.
- Training for prison warders should place emphasis on conflict resolution and respect for prisoners' rights rather than solely the enforcement of discipline.
- All alleged cases of abuse of the parole system by prison staff should be fully investigated and those involved disciplined. The criteria for early release or parole should be clearly explained to prisoners and uniformly applied across the system.

Integrated Reform

o An effort should be made to integrate reforms in the prison system with reforms in the general criminal justice system, so that, for example, efforts to reduce the prison population do not result in longer sentences being imposed by magistrates.

I. RECENT CHANGES IN PRISON LEGISLATION

Three of the most striking features of South African prisons were, until recently, the elaborate system of racial segregation, the strict secrecy surrounding prison matters, and the use of corporal punishment, sanctioned by law, as a disciplinary measure for infractions committed while in prison. With the political changes underway in South Africa in the last few years, some important legal changes affecting all three issues have taken place. In addition, South Africa has substantially revised the imposition of the death penalty and introduced a new non-custodial sentence of correctional supervision.

SEGREGATION

The first systematic efforts to segregate prisoners in South Africa along racial lines were made in the late nineteenth century. In 1911, after the creation of the Union of South Africa, the Prisons and Reformatories Act consolidated earlier colonial legislation, and strict segregation was enforced throughout the system. In 1959, major new legislation governing the prison service was passed by the National Party government. The Prisons Act reiterated the rules for segregation in prisons, in line with the policy of apartheid being enforced in all parts of South African life.[6]

The 1959 Prisons Act to some extent echoes the language of the Standard Minimum Rules for the Treatment of Prisoners, adopted by the U.N. in 1955. Rule 6(1) states that "The following rules shall be applied impartially. There shall be no discrimination on grounds of race, colour, sex, language, religion, political or other opinion, national or social origin, property, birth or other status." The South African government claimed that it was in conformity with this principle. Nevertheless, section 23(1) of the 1959 Prisons Act stipulated that, where whites and blacks were held in the same prison,

> (b) as far as possible, white and non-white prisoners shall be detained in separate parts thereof and in such manner as to prevent white and non-white prisoners from being within view of each other; and

---

[6]Van Zyl Smit, *Prison Law and Practice*, pp. 20-25.

(c) wherever practicable, non-white prisoners of different races shall be separated.

Prison regulations further mandated that white inmates be guarded solely by white prison personnel. Religious advisers catering to white inmates were also exclusively white. White prisoners were entitled to a different "diet scale" (the only black prisoners who received the same amount of food as white convicts were those on death row).

As part of the general retreat of South Africa from the laws implementing apartheid, prison regulations have undergone modifications since 1988, during which time all references to race have been removed.[7] In particular, amendments to the Prisons Act made in 1990 eliminated the requirement that white and black prisoners be housed separately by removing the provisions of Section 23 (1) of the 1959 Prisons Act quoted above.[8] The practical effect of the changes in the law and regulations are discussed in the chapter of this report on "Different Treatment Based on Race."

CENSORSHIP

Information about prison conditions was for many years closely guarded by South African government. In an attitude not unlike that of various communist governments, all matters related to prisons were deemed extremely sensitive. Prison-related issues were considered a matter of national security.

As one writer pointed out, this law meant that "those who question these aspects of our [South African] legal system may be accused of the worst crime of all — providing ammunition for the enemies of South Africa."[9] Despite these precautions, the international community continued to expose South African prisons for ill-treatment of prisoners and appalling working conditions. In the late 1950s and early 1960s, the

---

[7]*Ibid*, p. 39.

[8]Prisons Amendment Act 1990, section 10.

[9]S. Kentridge, "Telling the Truth about Law" (1982) *South African Law Journal*, 648, quoted in János Mihálik, "Restrictions on Prison Reporting: Protection of the Truth or Licence for Distortion?" *South African Journal on Human Rights*, (Capetown) Vol. 5, Part 3, 1989, p.410.

international campaign for the boycott of South African goods, later expanded by the anti-apartheid movement, began as a response to its prison system. South African prisons were repeatedly criticized by a number of human rights and international organizations. The government, for its part, alleged a "total propaganda war" by Amnesty International and the United Nations.[10]

The 1959 Prisons Act made it an offense to publish any false information on prisons, or, without the written authority of the Commissioner of Prisons, to publish other prison-related materials, including photographs or sketches of prisons or prisoners.[11] Even though Section 44(1)(f) of the Act proscribed only the publication of *false* information regarding prisons, it placed the burden of proof that the information was *not* false with the publisher. Because the courts tended to interpret this sub-section very strictly and lawsuits were costly and time-consuming, prison-related items virtually disappeared from the South African press for many years.[12] Furthermore, passing on information about prison conditions to even one more person was deemed to be in violation of Section 44. Consequently, even private correspondence on the subject was illegal.

---

[10]*Ibid*, p. 410.

[11]Section 44(1)(f) of the 1959 Prisons Act read, before it was amended: "Any person who publishes or causes to be published in any manner whatsoever any false information concerning the behavior or experience in prison of any prisoner or ex-prisoner or concerning the administration of any prison, knowing the same to be false, or without reasonable steps to verify such information (the onus of proving that reasonable steps were taken to verify such information being upon the accused); shall be guilty of an offense and liable on conviction to a fine not exceeding R.8,000 or, in default of payment, to imprisonment for a period not exceeding two years or to such imprisonment without the option of a fine or to both such fine and such imprisonment." Sections 44(1)(e) and (g) banned the taking or publication of photographs or sketches, and the publication of prisoners' own writings, respectively, without the written permission of the Commissioner of Prisons.

[12]Dirk Van Zyl Smit, "South Africa," in Dirk Van Zyl Smit and Frieder Dünkel (eds.), *Imprisonment Today and Tomorrow: International Perspectives on Prisoners' Rights and Prison Conditions*, (Boston: Kluwer, 1991), p. 546.

In 1984 the South African Minister of Justice agreed that the authorities would regard the requirements of the Prisons Act as having been met if the media submitted all reports to the prisons service before publication, and published, with equal prominence as the original report, any comments that the service might make.[13] This step did allow the South African media to give increased coverage to prison issues, but it was not until July 1992 that Section 44(1)(f) was repealed. Sections 44(1)(e) and (g), restricting publication of photographs and pictures of prisons, are still in force. In October 1992 a photographer for the Johannesburg *Weekly Mail*, a British reporter and a prisoners' rights activist were convicted of offenses including photographing prison installations and prisoners without permission, in connection with a *Weekly Mail* report on the use of the workshop at Leeuwkop prison, near Johannesburg, to manufacture weapons. The two South Africans were each sentenced to pay a R.1,000 (approximately $300) fine (the Briton had left the country).[14] Nevertheless, the Minister of Correctional Services recently insisted that the prohibition was not aimed at media reporting and was not "unqualifyingly prohibitive."[15] Some photographs of scenes inside prisons have recently been published in South African newspapers.

DISCIPLINARY MEASURES

Another important legislative change affecting prison conditions took place in mid-1993. Until that date, the list of sanctions for disciplinary infractions committed in prison included corporal punishment not exceeding six strokes, applicable for prisoners under forty years of age; and dietary punishment, consisting of reduced diet, usually in

---

[13] János Mihálik, "Restrictions on Prison Reporting," pp. 415-416; Dirk Van Zyl Smit "Helderstrom Prison, South Africa," in R. Whitfield (ed.), *The State of the Prisons* (London: RKP, 1989), p.70.

[14] Eddie Koch and Graham Harvey, "AWB uses prison as arms factory, claim warders," and Bafana Khumalo, "When going to jail is illegal," *Weekly Mail*, July 24 to 30, 1992 and October 23 to 29, 1992.

[15] Adriaan Vlok, quoted in "Media free to report on jail matters: Vlok," *Citizen*, May 6, 1993.

conjunction with solitary confinement.[16] These measures were exceptionally severe by international standards, and contrary to the U.N. Standard Minimum Rules. On June 23, 1993, an amendment to the Correctional Services Act was passed by Parliament which, among other things, removed corporal and dietary punishment as disciplinary measures.[17] Important new procedural protections regulating the implementation of the remaining disciplinary sanctions were also introduced. These reforms come into effect in March 1994. (See also the chapter on "Disciplinary Measures.")

Sentencing: The Death Penalty and Correctional Supervision

Until 1990, South Africa was among the world leaders in judicial executions. In 1987, 164 prisoners were hanged, the highest number ever.[18] However, on February 2, 1990 a moratorium on executions was announced in President de Klerk's speech opening the possibility of a negotiated transition to democracy.[19] New legislation reducing the number of capital crimes and providing increased protection for people accused of capital crimes was passed in July of the same year.[20] A review panel reconsidered death sentences passed before the legislative amendments, and had the power to commute them to a period of imprisonment. However, in a less positive development, executive control over sentences to life imprisonment was increased at the same time, with the initiative for release given only to the Commissioner of Correctional Services. Although no executions have taken place since 1989, the death

---

[16] Sections 51 and 54 of the Correctional Services Act prior to the June 23, 1993 amendment.

[17] Published in the *Government Gazette*, Vol. 336, No. 14889, Cape Town, June 25, 1993.

[18] János Mihálik, "The Moratorium on Executions: its background and implications," *South African Law Journal* Vol.108, Pt.1 (1991) 118-142; p.126.

[19] In fact, the last execution in South Africa was carried out on November 4, 1989; *Ibid*, p.118.

[20] The Criminal Law Amendment Act, 1990.

penalty is still imposed, and more than 300 people were still on death row at the end of 1993.[21]

In 1991, a new sentence of correctional supervision was introduced into the South African judicial system, under which convicted criminals may serve all or part of their sentences under supervision in the community rather than behind prison walls. Correctional supervision for a period of up to three years may be ordered by a court as an alternative to a custodial sentence or as a condition for the imposition of a suspended sentence. Alternatively, a prisoner may be released to serve out a sentence under correctional supervision after serving part of his or her or sentence in prison. By the end of August 1993, 6,433 prisoners had been sentenced directly to correctional supervision, and the sentences of 2,104 prisoners had been converted to correctional supervision. Although the new sentence is a positive development, several prisoners' rights activists expressed their concern to Human Rights Watch as to the manner in which the scheme was working in practice; in particular that the poor, especially those living in informal settlements, or squatter camps, did not benefit. Moreover, the numbers of convicted criminals sentenced to correctional supervision is not significant as a percentage of the total prison population. (See further, chapter on "Release.")

---

[21] In June 1993, South Africa's white parliament voted for an end to the moratorium; however, the government announced that no further executions would be carried out without consulting with other political parties, and in fact no moves to resume executions have been made. The ANC is opposed to the death penalty and has pledged to abolish it if, as is likely, it becomes the majority party in a new government.

II. PHYSICAL CIRCUMSTANCES

The total number of prisoners in South Africa, excluding the nominally independent homelands, stands at a daily average of approximately 110,000, with an annual turnover of 400,000. An additional 12,000 detainees are held in police lockups, according to the government.[22] Population statistics in South Africa are notoriously unreliable, but the population of South Africa excluding the homelands is estimated to be thirty-one million. The prisoner-to-population ratio from these figures is roughly 393 per 100,000. However, prison statistics for the "independent" TBVC states (Transkei, Bophuthatswana, Venda and Ciskei: together estimated to have a population of 7.5 million) are not easily obtainable, and could skew this ratio. Over recent years the number of prisoners fluctuated between about 100,000 in 1980 and the high of 118,000 in 1987.[23] At the end of 1991, following a large number of early releases, the figure temporarily dropped to 96,908 inmates.

OVERCROWDING

South African prisons are seriously overcrowded. In January 1993, the government stated that the prison system then held 110,000 prisoners in accommodations designed for approximately 84,000 (an overcrowding rate of 23 percent). This statistic, however, does not tell the whole story. The stated accommodation norms according to which a prison's capacity is measured, which were supplied to us by the Department of Correctional Services, are low to begin with: 61.04 square feet per prisoner in a single cell, and 38.86 square feet per prisoner in a communal cell.[24] Moreover, when discussing prison overcrowding it is

---

[22]*Beeld*, September 3, 1992, reprinted in FBIS-AFR-92-201, 16 October 1992; government press release January 6, 1993; letter from Department of Correctional Services to Human Rights Watch, June 15, 1993.

[23]János Mihálik, "The High Costs of Judicial Vengeance," *De Jure*, Vol.22 (1989), p. 41.

[24]The metric equivalents are 3.5m² per prisoner for a communal cell, and 5.5m² for a single cell. Rule 10 of the U.N. Standard Minimum Rules states, in very vague terms, that "All accommodation provided for the use of prisoners and

also important to remember that a prison that is filled at 100 percent of its capacity is in practice overcrowded. At any given time in any institution, some cells are not used for housing because they are being repaired, are temporarily used for storage or are not in use for other reasons.

Furthermore, some institutions are significantly more overcrowded than suggested by the national average. During our 1992 trip, we were told that the most overcrowded prison complex in the country was Pollsmoor. Even there, the level of overcrowding differed from prison to prison and two prisons within the complex were filled below their stated capacity. The numbers for the five facilities of Pollsmoor on the day of our visit there in August 1992 were as follows:

Maximum Security (Admission)	capacity	1,619
	number of inmates	3,192
Medium Security A	capacity	1,265
	number of inmates	1,893
Medium Security B	capacity	534
	number of inmates	684
Minimum Security	capacity	637
	number of inmates	522

---

in particular all sleeping accommodation shall meet all requirements of health, due regard being paid to climatic conditions and particularly to cubic content of air, minimum floor space, lighting, heating and ventilation." Regulation 97(1) of the Correctional Services Regulations, in words that closely follow Rule 10, provides that "No dormitory or cell shall be used for sleeping purposes unless it complies with the prescribed requirements in respect of floor space, cubic capacity, lighting, ventilation, and general health conditions." However, the relevant conditions, including space per prisoner, are "prescribed" not in the Regulations but in Departmental Orders, whose legal status is not clear. It is therefore extremely difficult both to find out the applicable norms, and especially to challenge actual conditions on their basis. See Van Zyl Smit, *Prison Law and Practice*, pp. 143-145.

Women's Prison	capacity	543
	number of inmates	340

The maximum security facility was almost 100 percent overcrowded. Yet even in the underpopulated "minimum security" prison (in practice a pre-release institution where prisoners served the last four months of their sentences) we observed cell overcrowding. The thirteen-inmate communal cells held fifteen prisoners, while cells down the hall stood empty.

At any given time, approximately 23 percent of inmates held by the South African prison system are pre-trial prisoners. Delay in the judicial process is one of the principal factors in overcrowding and, while most prisoners awaiting trial are brought to court within three months, some may remain in prison for over a year.[25] Nearly a quarter of prison space is therefore taken up by individuals who are legally still presumed innocent. Furthermore, under South African law, pre-trial detention does not automatically count towards the eventual sentence, although a judge *may* rule that credit for time served before the trial be given to the prisoner. Counting this time automatically into a final sentence would significantly reduce the overcrowding problem.

Prisoners awaiting trial receive better treatment than sentenced prisoners in some respects — for example, they may wear their own clothes and are allowed a greater number of visits. However, the overcrowding for prisoners awaiting trial may be worse and there are no opportunities for them to work. This lack of constructive activity is particularly problematic because pre-trial detainees are not classified in any way. During our prison visits, we encountered many indigent prisoners charged with non-violent offenses who were being held in

---

[25] As of December 31, 1991, 23,694 prisoners of a total prison population of 96,908 were awaiting trial. A government survey of all prisoners awaiting trial carried out on January 2, 1991, indicated that such prisoners had been held in custody as follows: one to fourteen days, 25.7 percent; fourteen days to one month, 30.5 percent; one to three months, 33 percent; between three and six months, 8.3 percent; longer than six months, 2.5 percent. However, in a survey of five urban prisons in February 1991, 16.29 percent of awaiting trial prisoners had been held longer than six months. Information given to Parliament by the Minister for Correctional Services, quoted in *SA Barometer* Vol.6, No.19, (Johannesburg) September 25, 1992.

custody only because they were unable to post bail, even of small sums. These prisoners were being held in the same accommodation as prisoners charged with violent crimes, to whom bail had been denied.

Attempts made by the government to address the question of overcrowding have included several amnesties. Common-law prisoners have benefited from successive general amnesties explicitly aimed to address overcrowding. Tens of thousands of prisoners were granted early release during 1991 and 1992, though most of them would have been released within a few months in any event. In January 1993, the government announced that the sentences of a further 7,500 prisoners would be remitted. In addition, approximately 1,600 political or security prisoners were released between February 1990 and late 1993.

TRANSFERS

Apart from early release, the only short-term measure used by the authorities to reduce overcrowding in a specific prison is the transfer of prisoners to less overcrowded prisons elsewhere in South Africa. Although this may be the best alternative under the circumstances, the attempts of the authorities to carry out such transfers lead to extreme discontent among the prisoners taken away from their home areas.

As part of a deliberate policy during the apartheid years, many prisons, particularly maximum security prisons, were located in remote rural areas. By their locations, escape was made more difficult, and the prisoner, isolated from his family, fell more totally under the control of the prison institution. Among the prisons we visited, Barberton prison complex, close to the border with Mozambique, was amongst the most notorious of these rural prisons, where conditions were often particularly harsh. As a consequence of this policy, South Africa lacks accommodation to house prisoners near to their home communities.

In every prison we visited that was not located in a major urban center, and in some others, prisoners complained to us that they were too far from home. Among current inmates, complaints about transfers far outnumbered complaints about any other aspect of prison life. Because of the cost and time of travel (Barberton is six hours by car, more by shared taxi, from Johannesburg, where a large number of its inmates have their homes), inmates of these prisons are almost certain to have few contacts with their families, or with the outside world in general. In some cases, prisoners stated to us that they could receive no visits at all because of the distance their families would have to travel. To a prisoner with no other connection to normalcy, this is an extreme hardship. Many told us that they preferred overcrowded cells to being far from their families.

In some cases, prisoners had taken extreme steps to force the authorities to agree to their requests to be transferred to a prison nearer to their families. In several cases, prisoners that we spoke to had mutilated themselves horribly with razor blades, leaving gruesome scars, or had threatened to commit suicide. Some of these had been charged with further offenses to add to their criminal record. Although, due to the location of many prisons, it would be impossible for the authorities to accede in the short term to all requests for transfers, many such requests seem to be unsympathetically rejected. Several prisoners and ex-prisoners quoted to us a saying reportedly often used by warders to prisoners asking to be moved: "This is the last station. You go nowhere from here."

CELL CONDITIONS

In the course of our two trips to South Africa, we visited over twenty prisons in ten prison complexes. We observed essentially two types of cells: single cells and the so-called communal cells, or dormitory-type cells.

At the time of our visits, single cells in men's prisons were used for three purposes: to house prisoners requesting separate accommodation, for example, in order to study, or for self-protection; for isolation for disciplinary purposes; and to segregate prisoners deemed to be violent or otherwise disruptive. Isolation as a disciplinary measure has now been abolished, effective March 1994.

Most single cells we visited measured approximately sixty square feet. When used by one prisoner, they seemed small but adequate in size. In some prisons, however, single cells are used to house three prisoners (the South African prison system, as a matter of policy, and in line with the U.N. Standard Minimum Rules, does not house two prisoners to a cell), making them extremely crowded. In the Pollsmoor maximum security prison, for example, a cell measuring fifty-six square feet housed three inmates, leaving barely enough room for the three of them to spread their sleeping mats.

The communal cells visited were of various sizes and held between ten and almost sixty prisoners. In one of the Brandvlei prisons, a cell of approximately 1,200 square feet held fifty-eight men on the day of our visit. A cell in Pollsmoor that measured 624 square feet, held thirty-five inmates. A 118-square-foot cell on death row in Pretoria Maximum Security prison could accommodate up to five inmates. These measurements gave a space per prisoner of respectively 20.6, 17.8, and 23.6 square feet, well under South Africa's stated norms.

Cell furniture in South African prisons ranges from spare to nonexistent. Many cells do not have beds, so that prisoners sleep on mats that are rolled up for the day. Lockers for private possessions are not standard, and where provided may be inadequate for the number of prisoners actually accommodated in the cell. Shelves, tables or chairs are also rare. For example, in single cells in the women's prison in Durban, we saw little desks, apparently for prisoners who were studying, but no chairs. However, in Kroonstad women's prison the cells were well-appointed with desks, chairs and shelves. Most dormitory cells had neither desks, nor chairs, nor tables.

One of the officials in Brandvlei prison said that even if the stated capacity of a communal cell was, for example, nineteen, and the cell held forty-one or forty-two people, there was "no problem with overcrowding" because double — and, in some cases, triple — bunks were in use. But the bunks we saw were low and there was not enough room to sit up on the lower one, making the cells extremely uncomfortable to live in, given the absence of other furniture.[26]

Most cells we visited had toilets, and communal cells had showers, usually shielded by a partition and sometimes located in an adjoining, separate room. In most cases, one toilet had to be used by as many as twenty people. Many cells smelled badly because of the presence or proximity of the toilet, coupled with bad ventilation. In Brandvlei, prisoners complained of cold in the winter and excessive heat during the summer months; in Barberton, in the sub-tropical "lowveld," prisoners from elsewhere in South Africa complained of the heat and humidity, convinced that it made them ill.

Light switches were outside the cell and were controlled by guards. In some prisons, for example on death row in Pretoria and in communal cells on Robben Island, lights were on twenty-four hours a

---

[26]In commenting on our report, the Department of Correctional Services denied that triple bunks were in use in South African prisons. We have, however, a photograph of triple bunks in use in a cell at Brandvlei prison. They also stated that the problem that bunks are low has been identified and would be addressed in the manufacture of new beds.

day. Some cells had insufficient natural light. For example, in the Modderbee prison, cells overlooking the road outside the prison had their windows blocked by louvre coverings, making the cells dark even during the day and preventing the prisoners from seeing outside.

Most prisons, with the notable exception of Pollsmoor Maximum Security, were exceptionally clean. Prisoners are required to work in maintenance of the facility and keep it in a spotless condition, as far as cleanliness is concerned. In prison after prison, we observed inmates polishing the floors to high luster, making the floors virtually dangerous to walk on. Cells in the majority of the prisons were also extremely neatly kept. Several prisoners, however, stated to us that prisons were abnormally clean in preparation for our visit.

In some cells in some prisons, male prisoners had painted the cell walls with elaborate murals on Biblical or other themes. In most cases, however, cells for male prisoners had no decoration, apart from elaborate fan-shaped and other compositions fashioned out of blankets and arranged on beds or sleeping mats, a unique form of prison art. In the hospital at Brandvlei, the wards were decorated almost as if for a Christmas party, with streamers and folded sheets. In Barberton Maximum Security prison, a cell for prisoners from the highest privilege group had a small area arranged with a display in tribute to the "Orlando Pirates" soccer team.

In women's prisons conditions were much more pleasant, although they varied considerably from one facility to another. In Kroonstad women's prison, which formerly held only whites, almost all inmates had single cells, whose doors were not individually locked. There were pictures on the hallway walls and in prisoners' cells, and plants in common areas. Many female prisoners had embroidered pillowcases or wall decorations for their individual cells, and most had bookcases, desks and chairs in their cells. By contrast, in Durban and Pollsmoor, women shared communal cells similar to those housing the male prisoners, though they suffered substantially less overcrowding. (See also the section on women in the chapter on "Special Categories of Prisoners").

BEDDING AND CLOTHING

Bedding differed from prison to prison. As mentioned above, in many prisons, especially in those formerly for black prisoners, there were no beds and prisoners slept on mats.[27] Even in those cells with beds, prisoners were not provided with sheets and pillows, nor with pajamas, and covered themselves only with blankets. Sheets and night wear were provided only to prisoners in hospital. Prisoners and former prisoners who had recently served time frequently reported that their blankets and bedding were infested with lice.[28]

Prisoners, except for judgment debtors and unsentenced inmates who are allowed to keep their own clothing, wear prison-issue uniforms. For men these are a standard dark green, sometimes threadbare and ill-fitting, but otherwise adequate, though some prisoners complained that in the extremes of summer and winter they were too hot or too cold.[29] Women also wear prison clothing, though it is less a uniform than a limited choice of prison-issue dresses. In Transkei, men's uniform was beige, and women wore a uniform of blue-gray dresses, with yellow headscarves. Prisoners may wear their own underwear. Prisoners are responsible for washing their own clothes and are issued laundry soap for this purpose, which must also be used for personal hygiene. Inmates complained that the quantity of soap was insufficient for frequent washes, and of poor quality.

FOOD

We received many complaints about food. Prisoners reported that food was of poor quality or insufficient in quantity, and that they often went hungry. Repeatedly, we heard of food served spoiled and of corruption in the kitchens, as a result of gang activity or with the

---

[27]The Department of Correctional Services stated to Human Rights Watch, commenting on our draft report in December 1993, that: "A comprehensive programme of providing beds to prisoners is at full swing at present."

[28]The prescribed hygiene requirements are that blankets and sleeping mats must be shaken out and aired once every two weeks, and that blankets must be washed twice a year; Van Zyl Smit, *Prison Law and Practice*, p.146.

[29]The Department of Correctional Services provided to Human Rights Watch a list of prison clothing available to sentenced prisoners, which "must, depending on work and current climatic conditions, be provided at the State's expense." Based on our interviews, however, it does not appear that the provision of clothing on this list is satisfactorily administered in all prisons.

collaboration of the warders. Many inmates pointed out to us that the last meal of the day was at 3:00 or 4:00 P.M. while breakfast was at 7 A.M., leaving them hungry for many hours. In some prisons, only two meals a day were served, and prisoners took bread and a drink with them to the cell as their third meal of the day. For example, in the Durban Westville prison complex, lunch was served at 12:30 P.M. At that time prisoners were issued bread and powdered drink for supper. Breakfast was at 7:30 A.M.

In most prisons, meals were served in dining halls. But in some, for example in the Pollsmoor Maximum Security prison, they were taken in the cells and had to be eaten in the presence of foul-smelling toilets, and often with nothing but the floor to sit on. We also heard complaints that spoons were often the only utensils issued to prisoners, regardless of whether they ate in dining rooms or cells, and that eating meals was difficult and unpleasant as a result.

Most food eaten by prisoners is grown on prison farms by prisoners themselves. In Brandvlei prison kitchen, our representatives were treated to a display of a veritable cornucopia of fruit and vegetables from the farm, allegedly for consumption by the prisoners. However, prisoners at Brandvlei and elsewhere complained that they rarely received fresh fruits or vegetables, and did not benefit from the agricultural work that they did. Prison farms do not sell their produce commercially, although it is available at below market prices to prison warders.

MEDICAL CARE

No medically-qualified individual was included among our representatives visiting South African prisons. Due to this lack of medical expertise, we did not focus on the quality of health care available to South African prisoners. Complaints about the lack of good health care were, however, very frequent. Most often these complaints referred to the cursoriness of medical examinations, especially of prisoners complaining that they should be exempted from working, and the tendency of the authorities to treat every prisoner making a complaint as a malingerer. Prisoners also stated that there were usually too many prisoners with complaints for the doctor to see in the time allocated.

Some prisons had their own in-house doctor; most prisons, however, were visited once or twice a week by doctors from nearby hospitals, and a doctor could be called at any time. All prisons we visited had qualified medical staff of some sort in residence. Clinics and wards that we visited were clean and apparently well-cared for; prisoners in the hospital were issued with sheets and pajamas, an unusual luxury.

Among the most frequent serious medical complaints we heard of were tuberculosis and asthma, clearly related to overcrowding. In these and other cases, prisoners received the appropriate drugs for free. Optical and dental care prescribed by a prison doctor on medical grounds are also free. However, in several cases prisoners stated to us that their requests for eyeglasses had been rejected as unnecessary, and that therefore they could not read.

Prisoners regarded as at a high risk of infection with HIV, the virus which causes AIDS — including drug addicts, those accused of sexual offenses and illegal immigrants from countries with a high incidence of HIV — are routinely given blood tests upon admission to the prison system. All prisoners working in the kitchen are also tested for the HIV virus. Prisoners known to be infected with HIV are segregated from the other prisoners at night, but not otherwise treated differently, according to prison staff. Despite the known high rate of homosexual behavior and sexual abuse in prison, condoms are not made available to prisoners to help reduce the spread of HIV infection.

III. DIFFERENT TREATMENT BASED ON RACE

Black male prisoners constitute the overwhelming majority of the South African prison population. As of December 31, 1992, the system held 4,258 white prisoners, of whom 191 were women. The total "non-white" prison population stood at 104,440, of whom 3,178 were women. The official statistics break down the "non-white" population into three racial groups: "Asian" (of Indian subcontinental ancestry), "Coloured" (mixed-race); and "Black." At the same date, the totals for each of the three groups were as follows: "Asian": 586; "Coloured": 27,315; "Black": 76,448.[30]

Some of the most significant variations in physical conditions arise from the different treatment of white and "non-white" prisoners. Apartheid in the prison system formally ended with amendments made to the Correctional Services Act in 1990. Gradually, some black, "coloured" or "Asian" prisoners have been placed in formerly all-white prisons and vice versa. The process has been slow, and at the time of our visits most prisons still had their "traditional" racial profiles, with only a small proportion of inmates of the other races. In particular, the formerly all-white prisons still had overwhelmingly white populations.

For example, at the Durban Westville prison complex, the formerly all-white prison, holding 229 inmates on the day of our visit, held 167 whites; while the three formerly black prisons, holding 2,507, 2,617, and 694 prisoners on the day of our visit, housed sixty-one, seventeen and twenty-seven whites, respectively. In the formerly all-white Pretoria Central prison, out of the population of 865, there were 674 whites on the day we visited. In Kroonstad Medium B prison, formerly housing only white men, there were 228 whites, seventy-two "coloureds" and 149 blacks in the prison on the day of our visit. Kroonstad Medium C, formerly used for white women, had achieved more balance: out of 147 prisoners, thirty-two were white, ninety-nine were black, and sixteen were "coloured."

The prisons that formerly housed no white prisoners continue to house mostly black prisoners. In the three Brandvlei prisons, holding a total of 2,532 prisoners on the day of our visit there in February 1993,

---

[30] Letter from the Department of Correctional Services to Human Rights Watch, April 2, 1993.

there were thirty-one white inmates. In the Barberton prison complex, also visited in February, there were two whites among the 3,780 inmates. In Kroonstad Medium A prison, formerly housing no white prisoners, there were only sixteen whites (described as "skollies" or hooligans by the commanding officer of the prison) among 1,115 sentenced prisoners. On Robben Island, a formerly all-black prison largely used for security prisoners, there were twenty-two whites out of the 615 prisoners on the day of our visit in August 1992.

The formerly all-white prisons had dramatically better living conditions. Even following the formal integration of the prison system, whites are usually afforded better treatment. We noticed that whites were often housed in single cells as opposed to communal ones (for example, on Robben Island virtually all the whites slept in single cells). Prison authorities, and some of the prisoners, stated that this housing pattern was the choice of the prisoners themselves. In addition, the formerly all-white prisons, where whites still account for the majority of inmates, tend to have single cells rather than dormitories. Where there are dormitories, whites are sometimes grouped together and do not share cells with non-whites. We also received reports that in some prisons beds were being introduced only after whites had been transferred to these institutions.

During several interviews we heard of different treatment being received by white and black prisoners. One of the most frequent complaints heard during our visits and in interviews with ex-prisoners was that white guards routinely used racial insults, and that both white and black warders were more likely to assault black prisoners and treat them more severely in all aspects of prison life. This type of discrimination is not officially permitted, but in practice prison warders face little threat of sanction. Although the display of political insignia is prohibited under the rules of the Department of Correctional Services, some prisoners reported to us that posters supporting white nationalist parties had been displayed in staff areas at election times.[31]

---

[31]In one particularly notorious case, it was alleged by Lawyers for Human Rights and others, based on evidence from prisoners and warders, that warders at Leeuwkop prison, near Johannesburg, were openly members of the paramilitary Afrikaner Resistance Movement (Afrikaner Weerstandsbeweging, or AWB) and were using the prison workshops to manufacture weapons which were then being used in township violence. The Department of Correctional Services denied that there was any AWB activity at the prison. Eddie Koch and Graham

Examples of official discrimination ranged from the relatively trivial — for example, at Brandvlei prison hospital, inmates reported that only whites got milk and that whites got different types of eating utensils — to the much more substantive. Several ex-prisoners complained to us that white prisoners would get additional time at visits, or would be allowed contact visits, when other prisoners in the same "privilege group" were not. They would also more quickly be promoted to the highest "privilege group", where they would avoid the worst hardships of prison. This differential treatment was also confirmed to us by some warders to whom we spoke outside prison walls, and by some white prisoners. In particular, whites have greater access to training facilities and are assigned to less onerous work. In prison after prison, we observed a high proportion of whites among prisoners employed in the kitchen (one of the most desirable work assignments in prisons worldwide); again, in workshops where inmates were receiving meaningful training, a disproportionate number of those benefiting were white. According to prison staff sources and prisoners themselves, white prisoners never work outside the prisons, in such facilities as police stations or courts or at other locations where they could be publicly seen. A white prisoner in Kroonstad complained that in fact this meant that blacks had more opportunities to see the outside world.

In some prisons, inmates were still segregated but appeared to be receiving similar treatment in other respects. In the women's prison at Kroonstad, a relatively pleasant environment for incarceration that had previously been used only for white women, black and white prisoners were housed in separate areas at night. However, all prisoners had single cells (which were not individually locked), and the conditions in the different areas appeared to be identical. The prison authorities justified the segregation on the grounds that, due to language problems, white and black prisoners wished to watch different television channels.

Some blacks held in formerly white prisons benefit from the historically better conditions afforded to whites; few whites are exposed to the worst prisons in the system. This observation appeared during our visits to apply particularly to juvenile prisoners: in no case did we see white juvenile prisoners being housed with black. On the other hand,

---

Harvey, "AWB uses prison as arms factory, claim warders," *Weekly Mail*, July 24 to 30, 1992.

although we did not visit any institutions designed for white children, we received reports that black children were being gradually introduced to these facilities.

Where whites have been introduced into historically black prisons, this has resulted in efforts to improve conditions; for example, by introducing beds. One case in which a white prisoner was placed in a formerly all-black prison among black prisoners led to an unsuccessful attempt to bring a court case challenging prison conditions. After Pollsmoor prison was integrated in December 1991, some white prisoners — until then used to what they had grown to consider the norm for prison conditions; that is, single beds with complete bedding, hot and cold water, adequate food, clean and vermin-free cells — suddenly, to their utmost shock, found themselves in what black prisoners had grown to consider normal. They were housed in cells that held twice the number of prisoners they were designed to house, and made to sleep on sleeping mats laid out on the floor, with two lice-infested blankets as bedding. Cells were dirty, damp, poorly lit, badly ventilated and with insufficient ablution facilities.

The newly transferred whites, along with their black fellow prisoners, who suddenly discovered that there could be better prison conditions within the same prison system, decided to challenge these conditions in court. (At the request of the attorneys for the plaintiffs, Human Rights Watch provided an affidavit describing the findings of our delegation's visit there in August 1992.) On the eve of the application, however, the prison authorities effectively put a stop to it by prohibiting legal consultations between the inmates and their attorneys and by transferring the would-be plaintiffs to different institutions.[32]

---

[32]South African law does not allow for class actions in the manner of the American system; such a case would have been exemplary only and required specific plaintiffs complaining at the specific conditions of their detention. In June 1993, the Department of Correctional Services commented that "The prisoners who allegedly planned the action against prison conditions indicated in a written affidavit that they were no longer interested in such a case. The allegation that the action was thwarted at the last minute by officials is rejected." Shehnaz Meer, "Bars to Exposing Conditions in Prisons," Supplement to the *Weekly Mail*, June 18 to 24, 1993. In an interview with Human Rights Watch, Shehnaz Meer, the attorney with the Legal Resources Centre (Cape Town) who attempted to bring this case, stated that the prisoners concerned had later

DISCRIMINATION AMONG PRISON STAFF

Until recent reforms, discrimination between black and white members of the prison staff was institutionalized in the same way as discrimination between black and white prisoners. For example, according to regulations replaced in 1990, all "white" members of the Department of Correctional Services automatically outranked all "non-whites."[33] Officially, there is now no discrimination in promotion, housing, or otherwise on racial lines among prison staff. A few black members of prison staff have reached high levels within the department: at Barberton prison complex, the head of the maximum security prison at the time of our visit, Colonel Khoza, was black. Shortly after our visit he was promoted to brigadier and became Commanding Officer of the Barberton prisons.

Nonetheless, as is the case with discrimination between prisoners of different races, informal discrimination continues. Many black or "colored" prison guards, speaking to us outside the prisons where they worked, said that promotion was routinely given to white warders over their colleagues, purely on racial grounds. Black warders also suffered discrimination in the allocation of housing to prison staff. Many of these guards were members of the Police and Prisons Civil Rights Union (POPCRU), an organization founded in 1989 by a group of "colored" policeman and prison guards which is committed to the improvement of working conditions for black and "colored" prison staff and to the promotion of respect for the civil rights of all prisoners and detainees. Individual members of POPCRU, and the organization itself, have been subject to official harassment.

The 1990 amendments to the prisons legislation, while repealing racially discriminatory provisions in the law, also made it an offense for members of the prison service to join or form a trade union without the permission of the Commissioner of Prisons. Although this measure was clearly aimed at POPCRU, the union continued to grow in strength,

---

informed her that the affidavits indicating that they were not interested in pursuing the case had not been voluntarily given.

[33] Regulation 3 (now amended); Van Zyl Smit, *Prison Law and Practice*, p.39.

especially among black police officers patrolling the townships.[34] In September 1993, legislation was finally passed to legalize unions in the prison service. The Department of Correctional Services stated to us in December 1993 that it "fully subscribes to the principles of freedom of association, of collective bargaining, as well as the universally acknowledged dispute resolution mechanisms."[35]

Several prison officers who were members of POPCRU stated that they had been subject to harassment by the authorities for their membership. Some had been subject to official disciplinary inquiries where they had been guilty of no misconduct, or of the same conduct as others who were not being investigated; other POPCRU members had been demoted, or given more onerous tasks within the prison system. In Pollsmoor prison complex, five guards lost their jobs in September 1992 for participating in a strike organized by POPCRU in 1990, and for their "poor career profiles."[36] One guard, also a founding member of POPCRU, was demoted and his pay reduced after it was discovered that he had been cooperating with our investigation of prison conditions.

In February 1993, over one hundred prison staff from Pietermaritzburg prison were dismissed, and approximately 200 others went on strike in sympathy. In March, seventeen POPCRU members from Pietermaritzburg, including the national Assistant General Secretary of the union, Zwi Mdletshe, were arrested for their activities in connection with the strike. Five were charged with the offense of

---

[34] In 1993, in response to widespread demonstrations by members of POPCRU, a new amendment to the Police Act empowered the Minister of Law and Order to promulgate regulations allowing union activity in the police force, although strikes would still be banned. A new union was formed at the same time, headed by conservative police officers. See, in particular, Paul Stober, "Conservative officers to form new police union," *Weekly Mail* September 17 to 23, 1993.

[35] Comments dated December 20, 1993, on the draft report on prison conditions prepared by Human Rights Watch, referring to the Public Service Labour Relations Act 1993.

[36] Terry Bell and Alex Dodd, "Popcru under pressure at Pollsmoor," *Weekly Mail* September 25 to October 1, 1992; comments of the Department to Human Rights Watch, December 20, 1993.

"intimidation." They were denied bail, according to the terms of the 1992 Criminal Law Amendment Act, which limited procedural protections for those accused of "special offenses," including intimidation. In May, after an expedited trial, all five were acquitted. All the dismissed warders, except Mdletshe, were eventually reinstated, following court action by POPCRU; Mdletshe was still under suspension at this writing, pending a hearing before a board of inquiry.

IV. THE "PRIVILEGE" SYSTEM

Almost anything an inmate is allowed to do or have in his or her possession is called a "privilege" or an "indulgence" in the South African prison system. Prisoners have few rights, and are entitled only to have those "privileges" granted to them by the Commissioner of Correctional Services at his discretion.

This philosophy, developed according to penal theories popular in the nineteenth century, was supported by South Africa's courts. For example, in one of the leading cases, *Goldberg v. Minister of Prisons*, the Appellate Division of the Supreme Court, the highest appeal court in South Africa, held that the rights of sentenced prisoners were limited to only those fundamental rights relating to their physical survival.[37] The attitude of the courts is likely to change dramatically once a justiciable bill of rights is introduced in South Africa, following the multiracial elections scheduled for April 1994. Support for prisoners' rights has already been significantly increased by the important case of *Minister of Justice v. Hofmeyr*. The Appellate Division affirmed the dissenting opinion of Mr. Justice (now Chief Justice) Michael Corbett in the *Goldberg* case, that "a convicted prisoner retains all the basic rights and liberties ... of an ordinary citizen except those taken away from him by law."[38] Despite this positive development in the law, the privilege system remains in place.

The detailed system by which privileges are allocated is set out not in the Correctional Services Act or in the regulations published with the legislation, but in Departmental Orders whose legal status is not clear.[39] As such, the content of the privileges that a prisoner may be awarded is in the sole discretion of the Commissioner of Prisons, beyond

---

[37] 1979(1)SA 14(A); see Van Zyl Smit and Dünkel (eds.), *Imprisonment Today and Tomorrow*, p. 542.

[38] 1993(3) SA 131 (A). The case dealt with the conditions of detention of a detainee under the emergency regulations, but the principles are equally applicable to those convicted of common crimes.

[39] Departmental Orders, Series B, V(3)(f)(i) to (xv); a copy of the list of privileges was supplied to Human Rights Watch by the Department of Correctional Services. See also Van Zyl Smit, *Prison Law and Practice*, p.193.

the reach of the courts.[40] All sentenced prisoners are allocated to one of four "privilege" groups, A, B, C or D. The privilege group to which a prisoner is assigned is unrelated to the length of his or her sentence or to perceived dangerousness, which are taken into account only in determining the classification into maximum, medium or minimum security prisons. All sentenced prisoners start out serving their sentences as members of group C, and Group A inmates tend to constitute a minority within each prison population. As of the end of July 1992, out of 241 sentenced prisoners in the female prison at Pollsmoor, there were 27 group A inmates; 38 group B; 172 group C and four group D. More than half the inmates were serving sentences of under two years, and of these, an overwhelming majority had classification C. On Robben Island, where sentences of up to ten years are served, out of 611 prisoners, 128 were group A; 177 group B; 303 group C and three group D.

Among "privileges" allocated according to a classification group are, most notably, the conditions regulating visits and telephone calls. We discuss these in detail in the chapter "Contacts with the Outside." Other "privileges" include: the right to sharing a meal during relatives' visits (only group A, since this is the one category of prisoner allowed any physical contact with visitors); purchases (the amount a prisoner is allowed to spend and the type of goods he or she may purchase vary according to classification); possession of musical instruments (group A only); writing of poetry (only groups A and B); hobbies (only groups A and B); possession of pets (group A only); television sets and cassette players in the cell (group A only); reading matter (group D is not allowed

---

[40] According to section 22(1) of the Correctional Services Act (as amended), "The Commissioner of Prisons shall determine ... (b) the groups into which prisoners are to be classified." Section 22(2) states that "The Commissioner may (a) grant such privileges and indulgences as he may think fit to any prisoner; (b) withdraw or amend any privilege or indulgence granted in terms of paragraph (a) to any prisoner if it is in the interests of the administration of prisons." The 1993 amendments to the Correctional Services Act removed the absolute discretion of the Commissioner to take away privileges from prisoners "notwithstanding anything to the contrary contained in any law ... [and] without furnishing any reason and without hearing such prisoner or any other person." However, there is still no right to a hearing when a prisoner is classified, nor is there any appeal from the decision.

to purchase any); library (group D one book a month, the other groups have unrestricted access and can borrow two books per occasion).

In addition to these different levels of "privilege" outlined by the regulations, different institutions have their own additional ways of rewarding those with the highest classification. For example, in the Pollsmoor female facility, group A prisoners had a separate dining room, nicer-looking than the one for the remaining prisoners. There is also a system of group privileges, by which, as a reward for good group behavior, all prisoners, irrespective of their individual privilege group, may be allowed to listen to music, enjoy extra recreational time and so forth.[41] Contrary to the U.N. Standard Minimum Rules, these privileges may be also removed as a form of group punishment.

A prisoner's performance is reviewed after three months and every six months thereafter by an "Institutional Committee," at which time he or she can be advanced one notch in the classification.[42] It thus takes a minimum of one year for a prisoner to reach the A group classification. But this can only happen if a prisoner has a spotless disciplinary record. Until the 1993 amendments to the prison legislation, demotions could happen at any time and were frequently used or threatened as a disciplinary measure; however, the new amendments provide that the reclassification of a prisoner's privilege group may not be used as a disciplinary measure (see further, chapter on "Disciplinary Measures").

The irony of the South African classification system is that it awards the best conditions to individuals who committed the most serious crimes, affording the harshest to those sentenced for the shortest terms. Only persons with relatively long sentences stand a chance of ever reaching the highest privilege group. Those with shorter terms will be out before they can get to the point in which they could have contact visits, for example.

---

[41] DOB V(3)(h)(i) to (vi).

[42] Section 62 of the Correctional Services Act, as amended. Subsections (2) and (3), added in 1993, provide that if a prisoner is not satisfied with the decision of the committee, he may submit a complaint, on the basis of which the commissioner may overturn the committee's decision. However, there is still no right to a hearing of any sort to challenge a prisoner's classification.

Prison Conditions in South Africa

In addition to the privilege system of groups A through D, some prisoners are designated as "monitors."[43] Monitors occupy the top of the prisoner hierarchy and are given jobs requiring some level of trust by the warders. For example, they may clean the staff offices or be entrusted with small amounts of money. During our prison visits, we encountered several such monitors clearly enjoying much more freedom to come and go around the prison grounds than other prisoners.

---

[43] DOB V(2)(d)(viii).

V. DISCIPLINARY MEASURES

One of the features of South African prisons that most strikes a visitor is the intense discipline inmates are living under. During our 1992 visits, in prison after prison, cell after cell, our representatives were greeted by rows of inmates, silently holding their I.D. cards just below their faces. At the time of our visits in 1993, there was less overt regimentation, but in many cases prisoners were clearly afraid of staff. Many inmates indicated their outright unwillingness to be interviewed, stating that they did not want to get in trouble; those who did agree to talk to us often expressed their fear of subsequent reprisals.

Despite the obvious emphasis on discipline, in none of the prisons visited were we able to ascertain that disciplinary rules were available to prisoners. When asked, prisoners told us that they never saw them. In Durban, prison officials told us that written rules were not issued to prisoners, though in other prisons we were assured that rules were available despite prisoners' denials. Section 85 of the Correctional Services Act states that the rules applicable to prisoners should be made available to every prisoner immediately after admission, or conveyed to him orally.[44] At our request, the Department of Correctional Services mailed to us the bilingual (English and Afrikaans) "Guide for Prisoners" containing excerpts from the Prisons Act and Prisons Regulations (as the legislation was previously known), but we never encountered a prisoner who had actually seen this document, and many expressed confusion as to the rules applying to them. Furthermore, the guide did not include any material from Departmental Orders, which contain many of the details

---

[44]This is in line with the U.N. Standard Minimum Rules, which provide, at Rule 35(1), that "Every prisoner on admission shall be provided with written information about the regulations governing the treatment of prisoners of his category, the disciplinary requirements of the institution, the authorized methods of seeking information and making complaints, and all such other matters as are necessary to enable him to understand both his rights and his obligations and to adapt himself to the life of the institution." In *Hassim v. Officer Commanding, Robben Island; Venkatrathnam v. Officer Commanding, Robben Island* 1973 3 SA 462 (C), the judge stated that "It is important that a prisoner know what his rights and duties are and it is therefore right and proper that he should have made available to him both the provisions of the Act and the regulations promulgated thereunder, which relate to the 'treatment and conduct of prisoners.'"

of the rules governing daily prison life. On a few occasions, we saw posted signs informing inmates or visitors what was prohibited, what were the limits on the money in possession of inmates in each privilege group or the number of photographs an inmate might have in his or her cell.

In addition to their ignorance of the centrally authorized rules governing everyday life in the prisons, some inmates complained they did not know how the "privilege" classification system worked, or that they did not believe they should be under a specific privilege classification and could not get an explanation from the authorities as to why they had been allocated to one level rather than another.

AUTHORIZED MEASURES

Sanctions that may be applied to prisoners for disciplinary infractions are set out in the Correctional Services Act and in regulations made by the Minister of Correctional Services under the act.[45] As an overall rule, it is stated in the regulations that "discipline and order shall be maintained with firmness but in no greater measure than is necessary for security purposes and an orderly community life in a prison;" and that "the aim in treating the prisoner shall at all times be to promote his self-respect and to cultivate a sense of responsibility in him."[46]

Despite these sentiments, South African prisons have historically authorized exceptionally brutal punishment, in comparison to international standards. A wide range of petty disciplinary infractions are criminalized under the legislation, and were punishable by measures going well beyond accepted norms, including dietary and corporal punishment. However, several of the harshest disciplinary sanctions, which were still lawful at the time of our 1992 and 1993 visits, were legally removed with the June 23, 1993 amendment to the Correctional Services Act. The amendments do not come into effect until March 1994,

---

[45]The rules for trial of offenses under the act or the regulations, and the types of punishment that may be imposed on prisoners, are set out in sections 51 and 54 of the Correctional Services Act. Section 94 sets out the Minister's powers to make regulations.

[46]Correctional Services Regulations, regulation 98(1). This wording echoes that of the U.N. Standard Minimum Rules, which provide, at Rule 27, that "Discipline and order shall be maintained with firmness, but with no more restriction than is necessary for safe custody and well-ordered community life."

and the punishments to be abolished were still being applied at the end of 1993. (See further, the chapter on "Legislative Changes").

Prior to the changes, offenses set out in the act itself were punishable, after trial by a magistrate, by a sentence of up to six months' (additional) imprisonment, or by "solitary confinement in an isolation cell with or without light labour for a period not exceeding forty-two days, twenty-eight days of which may be ordered to be passed on reduced diet." Such trials would usually take place in specially designated courtrooms in the prison itself; only more serious offenses, also crimes under legislation not concerned specifically with offenses in prison, would be tried in a court outside the prison. The prisoner had a right to legal representation in either case; however, almost no prisoners in fact have legal assistance if they are charged with further offenses (80 to 90 percent of those charged with criminal offenses outside prison are unrepresented at trial). Punishments for contraventions of the regulations alone could be imposed by any designated commissioned officer, without a right to appeal his decision. Possible sentences that could be imposed, and which were also available to the magistrate, included the deprivation of one or more meals on any day; corporal punishment "not exceeding six strokes" for a male prisoner under forty years of age; and solitary confinement for up to thirty days, again with or without dietary restrictions.

The authorized thirty days of dietary punishment for violations of the regulations consisted of eighteen days of "spare diet," six days of "reduced diet," and six days of full diet.[47] A spare diet was described in detail by the regulations as "200 grammes of maize meal, twice daily, boiled in water without salt, and 15 grammes of protone soup powder, boiled in 570 millilitres of water, once daily."[48] Reduced diet, according to the regulations, consisted of "half of the prescribed daily ration."[49] The twenty-eight days of reduced diet imposable by a magistrate were subject to the limitation that no more than fourteen days of reduced diet

---

[47] Correctional Services Act, Section 54(e), now amended.

[48] Correctional Services Regulations, Regulation 101(b), now amended.

[49] *Ibid*, Regulation 101(c), now amended.

could be served in one stretch, and fourteen days had to intervene between each period of reduced diet.[50]

During our visits in 1992 and early 1993 we saw punishment cells in use in a number of prisons. Most were single cells, with no furniture except a toilet and sink, and only mats on the floor to sleep on. Prisoners in punishment were not allowed any books except the Bible. Many of those we interviewed who were being punished by solitary confinement were also subject to dietary punishment, making the prisoner go hungry for a day, or subjecting him to the more elaborate regime set out for longer periods. Offenses being punished included swearing, being found in possession of marijuana, or fighting with fellow prisoners.

Statistics given to Parliament by the Department of Correctional Services concerning disciplinary measures indicate that dietary punishment was frequently used as a sanction in the South African prison system until the recent legislative changes. However, its use did appear to be declining, even before the reforms. As a result of court supervision which severely restricted its application, corporal punishment was little used in recent years. The figures are shown in the table below:[51]

Year	Deprivation of one or more meals on any given day	Use of corporal punishment (up to six lashes)
1989	35,805	120
1990	32,963	102
1991	27,930	44
1992	29,063	41

The amendments introduced in June 1993 removed the sanctions of corporal and dietary punishment and solitary confinement with or without restraint, as disciplinary measures, bringing South Africa into line

---

[50]*Ibid*, Regulation 51(2)(b), now amended.

[51]*SA Barometer*, Volume 6, Number 19, September 25, 1992, and *SA Conflict Monitor*, (Johannesburg) March 1993, quoting statistics given by the Minister of Correctional Services to Parliament.

with the U.N. Standard Minimum Rules.[52] Additional imprisonment of up to six months may still be imposed by a magistrate for contraventions of the act and, in substitution for the sentence of solitary confinement, a magistrate will be able to sentence a prisoner "to pay partial or full compensation for any damage caused by the misdemeanour of which he has been found guilty." The imposition of disciplinary sanctions for contravention only of prison regulations is given to an "institutional committee," consisting of an unspecified number of warders designated for that task; rather than, as before, to a single commissioned officer. After a hearing (at which a right to legal representation is specifically excluded), the committee may order that the prisoner be deprived for up to two months of "one or more privileges or indulgences."[53] A change in the general classification of the prisoner under the privilege system is specifically excluded as a disciplinary measure; and the prisoner is "at all times [to] be entitled to maintain his family ties."[54]

Despite these reforms, the privilege system itself and the general treatment of all amenities, barring those essential for the physical survival of the prisoner, as "privileges or indulgences," allow an unacceptable level of discretion to prison guards in determining the living conditions of those under their supervision. Prisoners may be deprived as a disciplinary measure of study opportunities, reading material, pens and paper, personal possessions such as watches, even (as we were told by prisoners in isolation cells in Kroonstad) belts and blankets. Under Section 22 of the Correctional Services Act, before the recent amendments, it was

---

[52] Rule 31 of the U.N. Standard Minimum Rules provides that: "Corporal punishment, punishment by placing in a dark cell, and all cruel, inhuman or degrading punishments shall be completely prohibited as punishments for disciplinary offences." Rule 32(1) permits punishment by reduction of diet provided "the medical officer has examined the prisoner and certified in writing that he is fit to sustain it."

[53] Under the U.N. Standard Minimum Rules, Rule 30(2) states that "No prisoner shall be punished unless he has been informed of the offence alleged against him and given a proper opportunity of presenting his defence. The competent authority shall conduct a thorough examination of the case."

[54] Correctional Services Amendment Act 1993, Sections 16 and 17, amending Sections 51 and 54 of the principal act.

explicitly stated that privileges could be withdrawn from any prisoner "notwithstanding anything to the contrary contained in any law," and "without furnishing any reason and without hearing such prisoner or any other person." Although this section was amended in 1993 to restrict the withdrawal of privileges to cases in which "it is in the interests of the administration of prisons," it is not clear what difference this rewording will make in practice.[55]

The long list of disciplinary infractions for which a prisoner may be punished under the regulations remains unchanged by the recent amendments to the act. The list covers a range of misdemeanors, some potentially serious but many trivial. They include willfully giving false replies to questions put by a warder; disobeying lawful commands given by a warder; "petty assault;" swearing; singing, whistling, or making "unnecessary noise;" shirking work "in any manner," or acting "in any manner ... contrary to good order and discipline."[56] Perhaps most troublingly, the list also includes lodging "false, frivolous or malicious complaints," or making "false and malicious accusations against a member [of the prison staff], a fellow prisoner or other person."[57] In the same way as the now-removed provisions in the Correctional Services Act that made it illegal to make any false statement about prisons had a chilling effect on the press and essentially eliminated any coverage of prisons from South African media, these rules discourage prisoners from making any complaints, either about conditions in general or against staff members. Prisoners and ex-prisoners we interviewed frequently stated that they were punished for complaining to warders, or for making requests such as for a transfer to a different prison.

The reforms to disciplinary measures introduced by the Correctional Services Amendment Act of 1993 are welcome and long overdue. They are not yet in effect, and will be introduced gradually by executive order. The reforms relating to punishment for disciplinary offenses are to become effective in March 1994.

---

[55] Section 8, Correctional Services Amendment Act, 1993, amending Section 22 of the Correctional Services Act, 1959.

[56] Correctional Services Regulations, Regulation 99, (a), (b), (e), (i), (q), and (u).

[57] Correctional Services Regulations, Regulation 99 (o) and (p).

However, we observed during our visits a confusion between the use of sanctions such as solitary confinement for punishment, and the use of these sanctions as a means of "restraining" violent or otherwise abusive prisoners, that may allow their continuing use effectively to punish prisoners even when the recent reforms come into effect.[58]

Section 80 of the Correctional Services Act allows the head of a prison to order a prisoner to be "confined in an isolation cell, and, in addition or in the alternative, if necessary, to be placed in irons or subjected to some other approved means of mechanical restraint for such period as may be considered absolutely necessary, but not exceeding one

---

[58]In *Hassim v. Officer Commanding, Robben Island; Venkatrathnam v. Officer Commanding, Robben Island* 1973 3 SA 462 (C), a leading case on prison conditions, the judge emphasized that it was of "fundamental importance" to maintain the distinction between "solitary confinement" used as a punishment, and "complete segregation" used to maintain "good order and discipline" in the prison. See Van Zyl Smit, *Prison Law and Practice*, p.70. Regulation 102 of the Correctional Services Regulations also states that restraint "shall in no circumstances whatsoever be used as a punishment." Both the case law and the regulation conform to the U.N. Standard Minimum Rules, which provide, at Rule 33, that

> Instruments of restraint such as handcuffs, chains, irons and straitjackets, shall never be applied as a punishment. Furthermore, chains or irons shall not be used as restraints. Other instruments of restraint shall not be used except in the following circumstances: (a) As a precaution against escape during transfer, provided that they shall be removed when the prisoner appears before a judicial or administrative authority; (b) On medical grounds by direction of a medical officer; (c) By order of the director, if other methods of control fail, in order to prevent a prisoner from injuring himself or others or from damaging property; in such instances the director shall at once consult the medical officer and report to the higher administrative authority.

Rule 34 provides that

> The patterns and manner of use of instruments of restraint shall be decided by the central prison administration. Such instruments must not be applied for any longer time than is strictly necessary.

month." The period of such isolation or restraint may be extended for up to three months by the Commissioner of Correctional Services, and indefinitely by the Minister. In addition, Sections 78 and 79 (as amended), state that prisoners may be "segregated" in isolation cells if it is "desirable in the interests of the administration of justice," or in order to ensure that other disciplinary measures can be "effectively applied." Segregation in this way is "not to be deemed to be solitary confinement" for the purposes of punishment.[59]

We interviewed prisoners held in isolation cells in several prisons, including prisoners subject to restraint, who were completely unaware of any distinction between isolation as a punishment and isolation as a means of ensuring good order in the prison. From the point of view of the individual prisoner, the difference between the two types of isolation is purely academic. Moreover, there appears to be a similar confusion in the minds of at least some of the warders. In Brandvlei maximum security prison, for example, a warder questioned about the status of prisoners being held in single cells stated that the prisoners were in isolation because they had committed disciplinary offenses. When asked how long their sentences were, the warder stated that there was no maximum, the length of time spent in isolation depending on the behavior of the prisoner. Solitary confinement described as a punishment was being viewed not as a fixed sentence but as something conditional upon the prisoner's behavior; meanwhile, the theoretical time limits

---

[59]Regulation 118 of the Correctional Services Regulations authorizes the segregation of prisoners by the Commissioner "when a prisoner has a bad or harmful effect on another prisoner or is responsible for the deterioration of the relationship between a member and a prisoner and their attitudes towards each other, or causes unrest or dissatisfaction among other prisoners or incites other prisoners to submit trivial or untrue complaints and representations or incites or influences other prisoners to disregard or contravene any command or instruction or tries to do or bring about any of the aforementioned, or has attempted to escape, or when there are reasonable grounds for believing that he is planning to escape, or when such prisoner has again been taken into custody after escape from prison or other lawful detention, or becomes violent or adopts a threatening or aggressive attitude towards a member or temporary warder or any other prisoner or person, or conducts himself or acts in any manner which conflicts with the good order and discipline of the prison."

provided under the act, either for punishment or for restraint, were apparently not regarded as binding.

Two recent inquests into deaths in prison confirm this confusion and the serious consequences it may have. In January 1993, a magistrate conducting an inquest into the death in June 1989 of Carol Anne Meyers, a twenty-year-old woman, found that her death was caused by the "irresponsible and inhuman" conduct of prison officers applying restraint under Section 80. Meyers died as a result of injuries incurred from being kept in a straitjacket for twenty-three hours by warders in Pollsmoor prison. She had been placed in a straitjacket after she had threatened to commit suicide. The court found that prison regulations had been disregarded in applying the restraint, and also that warders had regarded the restraint as a punishment. Both officers involved were promoted after the death occurred. Similarly, an inquest into the death in June 1991 of Johannes Oor, discovered hanged in his cell eight days after he had been ordered confined to one month's isolation, found that Section 80 had been misapplied.[60] The Minister of Correctional Services stated in March 1993 that straitjackets had been used sixty-one times in South African prisons during 1992.[61] However, later in the year it was announced that the use of straitjackets would be drastically curtailed.[62]

Contrary to the U.N. Standard Minimum Rules, collective punishment for group misbehavior is authorized by Departmental Order.[63] During the course of our visits we received several reports of

---

[60] Donald Zake, "Death jacket: Still no action," *South*, (Cape Town), February 13 to 17, 1993; Sandy Liebenberg, "Protecting people's rights even behind prison bars," *Weekly Mail* Supplement, June 18 to 24, 1993.

[61] *SA Conflict Monitor*, March 1993.

[62] On August 30, 1993, the Department of Correctional Services announced that in future straitjackets would be fitted after examinations of a prisoner by a doctor and psychiatrist, and that a prisoner subject to such restraint would be examined at least every hour. *SA Conflict Monitor*, August 1993.

[63] The order states, "When group punishment is necessitated to maintain sound discipline due to the actions or behavior of a group of prisoners, if it is impossible to identify the guilty among them, the Commanding Officer may order that all or some privileges or indulgences are to be withdrawn for at most

collective punishment. In Modderbee prison, for example, inmates told us that if there was a fight, everyone was punished, even those who were not involved. The usual punishment was lockdown in the cells, with only thirty minutes of exercise a week. Similarly, we were told by the Barberton prison inmates that the Sunday soccer game was frequently cancelled if anyone misbehaved. In addition, soccer games were stopped in one section of Barberton altogether at the time of our visit because of gang-related violence. All prisoners in the section, regardless of whether they had engaged in gang activities, were affected by this sanction. In the Kroonstad male prison, inmates reported that in November 1992 two prisoners threw porridge on the floor because they wanted to see an officer to report a complaint. All prisoners present in the room were punished with the loss of three meals, reduction of blankets and were placed in restraints.

UNAUTHORIZED MEASURES

As mentioned above, most prisoners were not eager to provide testimonies as to the use of punishment and indicated their fear of reprisals. Some, however, did agree to talk while in prison; ex-prisoners also spoke to us about the unauthorized use of punishment. In addition, some prison guards gave testimony, outside the prison walls, about the behavior of their fellow warders.

In some cases, we were told of authorized means of punishment extended to an illegal degree or used for illegitimate purposes. On at least two occasions, we received testimonies of solitary confinement with reduced diet being used for up to sixty days, despite the legal limit of thirty or forty-two, depending on the infraction.[64] In Barberton,

---

72 hours." DOB V(3)(k)(iv); see also Van Zyl Smit, *Prison Law and Practice* pp. 194-5. Collective punishment is contrary to the U.N. Standard Minimum Rules. Rules 27 to 32 set out standards applying to punishment, which provide for procedures for individuals to be heard and given an opportunity to state a defense in every case.

[64] In commenting on our draft report, the Department of Correctional Services stated that it can happen that a prisoner can receive two different sentences of solitary confinement with dietary punishment for two different offenses, totalling more than thirty days. In such cases, however, an interval of at least fourteen days, or as directed by the medical officer, is prescribed between

prisoners complained about the use of isolation cells as punishment for requesting transfers to different prisons, or for making complaints about the food. In the Kroonstad male prison we received two separate yet similar testimonies from black prisoners who were in solitary confinement for having a fight. Each of them had fought with a white inmate. They alleged that the white prisoners were not in punishment.

Although the threat of reclassification within the privilege system was not authorized as a disciplinary measure at the time of our visits, we received several reports of cases in which reclassification of prisoners under the privilege system or by security status had in fact been threatened or carried out. Moreover, since each prisoner is subject to potential reclassification every six months, it is not clear that the addition of a specific prohibition of reclassification of a prisoner under the privilege system as a disciplinary measure, introduced by the 1993 amendments, will mean that reclassification will not continue to be used effectively as a punishment. It will still be open to warders to threaten a prisoner with downgrading of privilege group in retaliation for disciplinary offenses.

Many prisoners and ex-prisoners alleged that they were subject to reprisals for making complaints. In Barberton, a prisoner complained that he had been transferred to the maximum prison from the medium after going on a hunger strike to protest the failure to respond to his requests for a transfer. His books and writing materials were confiscated, and he spent some time in the isolation cells. On January 22, 1993 he was assaulted by a warder, in front of a superior officer, while asking about his security classification. The prisoner made a complaint about this treatment, and was told that it was up to the commanding officer of the prison to decide whether to bring in the police to lay a charge against the warder concerned. At the date of our visit, one month later, no action had been taken other than to take a statement from the prisoner for the purposes of the disciplinary committee. Another prisoner facing further charges for attempted suicide stated that his injuries had been caused by warders who had pushed his hands through a window after he had complained about the behavior of a member of prison staff.

In several other testimonies, inmates described acts of violence inflicted by prison officials. In the Modderbee prison, inmates said that

---

the serving of each sentence.

guards often beat prisoners in retaliation for infractions, real or imaginary, sometimes inflicting serious injuries. One inmate was beaten on February 16, a few days before our visit, for putting his clothes outside the cell window. A prisoner at Pollsmoor complained about an assault by a warder the previous October, and stated that no statement had ever been taken. In Modderbee prison, we interviewed juvenile prisoners who stated that the warders at the prison would sometimes assault them, and that they feared that the warders observing our consultations would assault them for talking to our representative.

In Barberton we received numerous reports of staff assaults against prisoners, including beatings with a *sjambok* (rawhide whip) and beatings in isolation cells, as an additional punishment on top of solitary confinement. In Kroonstad male prison, we were also told about beatings in isolation cells. An ex-prisoner from Leeuwkop described a "seven-day punishment," in which a prisoner would be put in an isolation cell for one week and be assaulted every day. An ex-prisoner who had spent time in Groenpunt reported to us that he had been assaulted in August 1992 by the head of the prison after his father had threatened to bring a case against the prison in connection with another charge against the prisoner. He had been beaten with batons for forty-five minutes in an isolation cell, and had been told to plead guilty in the other case (which was eventually dropped). He had not taken any action as a result of the assault because he had only three months left to serve of his sentence and was afraid of causing trouble. He stated: "They assault you no matter what you do. If you are right, if you are wrong, they just assault you."

Some testimonies regarding violence inflicted by prison staff members on inmates come from concerned staffers, often members of POPCRU, the Police and Prisons Civil Rights Union. A Pollsmoor sergeant described an incident in which prisoners were beaten by staff members after the inmates had allegedly assaulted an officer. In a sworn affidavit provided to the prisoners' lawyers, the sergeant recounted the events that occurred on October 1, 1992 and stated: "I proceeded down to A Section [of the Maximum prison at Pollsmoor] where I witnessed seven or eight fellow warders (*inter alia* Warder Le Roux and Sergeant Langberg) repeatedly assaulting four or five prisoners who had allegedly been responsible for stabbing Warrant Officer Murray. In my assessment of the situation these assaults were unnecessary as by the time I arrived in A Section W/O Murray had been removed and weapons confiscated. The repeated assaults were excessive."

In another affidavit, a different sergeant described his visit with one of the victims of the same incident: "Amongst the prisoners who have been placed in solitary confinement is John Odendaal. I have spoken to him and he informed me that he was assaulted. At the time when I spoke to him I noticed a large wound on the back of his head, which appeared to be recently inflicted. Prisoner Odendaal was also depressed and on the verge of bursting into tears when I spoke to him. He is quite a frail man and uses a walking stick to support a bad leg."

It is certain that in the vast majority of cases warders who assault prisoners receive no punishment, nor the victim any compensation. Many prisoners stated to us that they had not even lodged an official complaint with the authorities if they had been assaulted, either fearing reprisals or believing that it was useless. In May 1992, the Minister of Correctional Services stated that 1,426 complaints against warders had been lodged by prisoners during 1991; sixty-three warders had been charged as a result of these complaints, and twenty-four had been found guilty of assault.[65] In March 1993, the minister stated that 1,482 complaints of assault were lodged in 1992, six warders were convicted of criminal charges, and twenty-eight disciplined within the department.[66] In May 1993, the minister gave official statistics for deaths in prison during 1992: according to the department, a total of 202 prisoners died, 140 of natural causes, thirty-six suicides, thirteen assaulted by fellow prisoners, and thirteen of various causes including drowning, falling from prison vehicles, and a prison accident.[67]

Although criminal prosecution of warders for assault is within the discretion of the authorities, a prisoner may independently bring a civil claim for damages against an individual warder and the prison service. One of the principal restrictions on bringing such actions are the extremely short limitation periods within which a claim must be brought under South African law. Under the Correctional Services Act, a prisoner must bring an action based on anything done to him in prison within six months of his release, and in any event not more than one year after the

---

[65] *SA Barometer*, Volume 6, No. 9, September 25, 1992.

[66] *SA Conflict Monitor*, March 1993.

[67] *SA Conflict Monitor*, May 1993

incident occurred.[68] This provision seriously reduces the chances that a warder guilty of assault will ever be made accountable for his action. In any event, since most prisoners will seek legal advice only once they have been released, it restricts possible civil actions for damages to assaults taking place during the prisoner's last year in custody.

MISTREATMENT OF PARTICIPANTS IN NON-VIOLENT PROTESTS

As mentioned before, as a result of political agreements and also in an effort to relieve overcrowding, several amnesties were promulgated in South Africa, both for political and for nonpolitical prisoners. Many prisoners excluded from these releases engaged in protest actions, including hunger strikes. We received disturbing testimonies about the treatment afforded to participants in some of these fasts.

In May 1991, after the expiration of the April 30 deadline for the release of political prisoners which had been agreed between the government and the ANC, a group of inmates of Barberton prison who claimed political status embarked on a hunger strike. The prison administration tried to put pressure on the strikers to end their protest. At one point, the guards took away all their clothing and other belongings and prisoners remained completely naked for an entire night. The next morning the clothes were returned and the prisoners were taken to the prison hospital and placed in the mortuary. The prisoner who provided the testimony to us said that he was very cold in the morgue. That inmate was released from prison after twenty-seven days of his hunger strike. Another prisoner participating in the same protest was taken to an outside hospital after eighteen days of a hunger strike. Until a visit from his lawyer, the prisoner alleged that he had been chained to his bed by his hands and his legs, and later by his hands only.

As a result of this treatment of hunger-striking prisoners, the doctor who had been responsible for their treatment was investigated for malpractice by the South African Medical Council. In March 1993, the council found that there was insufficient evidence to justify a finding of malpractice.

---

[68]Correctional Services Act, section 90. In addition, one month's notice in writing must be given to the defendant before the action is commenced, reducing the limit to an effective five months.

VIOLENCE IN THE AFTERMATH OF A PRISON RIOT

The expectations and tensions related to anticipated releases of common crime prisoners led to a violent protest in Barberton in August 1991. Prisoners burned their cells in order, as one of the protest's participants explained to us in 1993, "to get attention." After the fire and the protest were subdued, six prisoners were dead. The official version is that they died in the fire. But several prisoners interviewed by us who said they witnessed the events stated that the six were killed by the prison staff. As one prisoner stated to us: "They were brutally murdered by the prison members accompanied by the top officers. They trapped them with their boots on their stomachs, and beat them and pulled them along the floor to B section hospital. When they reached the hospital, some of them were still alive." Another described the incident as a "festival of bestial brutality and terror."

One prisoner, who was being held in an isolation cell at his own request, stated that he had been in the cell where the prisoners had died. He stated that one of the prison officers had used a hose to drive the prisoners out of the toilet area of the cell, where they were sheltering from the fire that they had lit, rather than spraying the fire itself. As a result the six prisoners had died. Another prisoner stated that when he and others were charged with a further offense as a result of being participants in this action, they had been assaulted by warders. When they asked to give a statement to the police about this assault and identified the warders involved, the prison authorities offered them a "settlement" by which they would be given remission of sentence and desirable work assignments if they would drop the charges. He had refused to do so.

Later in the year, after our visit to Barberton, fifteen prisoners, including several that we had spoken to, were charged with murder and manslaughter in connection with the deaths of the six prisoners during the riot. A *pro deo* counsel was appointed by the state on their behalf, as is the custom for capital offenses. However, no full and independent inquiry has been held into the events leading to the deaths, and no disciplinary action has been taken against any of the warders alleged by the prisoners to have been involved in the incident.

VI. GANGS AND VIOLENCE

Prison life in South Africa is characterized by an elaborate system of gangs, through which much prisoner-on-prisoner violence is mediated. While gang activity is common to many prison systems, South African prison gangs are distinctive. Most importantly, gangs in South African prisons have a national organization, and a gang member who is transferred from one prison to another, or even released and reimprisoned, will keep his membership and gang rank in the new prison. The gangs have a history that predates the formation of the South African prisons department. They are not spontaneous creations in each prison, with an improvised system of membership and command, but have an elaborate structure, ranking and disciplinary code that mimics the militaristic structures of the South African apartheid system in general and the prison administration in particular.

The three predominant gangs operating in South Africa's prisons today are the 28s, 27s and 26s, known collectively as the "number gangs." They trace their origins, by an elaborate oral history, to the late nineteenth century, when gangs were formed in the all-male compounds occupied by migrant laborers working in the mines on the Witwatersrand, near Johannesburg. One man, Nongoloza Mathebula (1867-1948), is credited with the establishment of the basics of the gang system. Gang membership spread from the mining compounds to the prisons, aided by South Africa's pass laws, which ensured that the great majority of black South African males were exposed to the criminal system, since they could be arrested at any time for failure to carry documentation proving their right to be in a particular place. By the 1920s, the gangs had ceased to exist in their original form outside the prisons, but had become entrenched inside the prison walls.[69]

Each of the gangs has an elaborate quasi-military command structure, involving up to thirty different ranks; each rank has specific hierarchical duties, and internal discipline is strictly maintained. Promotion, particularly to the higher ranks, may be obtained by

---

[69]Nicholas Haysom, *Towards an understanding of prison gangs*, Institute of Criminology, University of Cape Town, 1981; M. Slabbert and J.H. van Rooyen, *Some implications of tattooing in and outside prison*, Institute of Criminology, University of Cape Town, 1978; Van Zyl Smit, *Prison Law and Practice*, pp. 48-50.

committing acts of violence on persons outside the gang. The gangs themselves are distinguished according to their aims and activities: the 28s are regarded as the senior gang, and are distinguished primarily by their organized system of "*wyfies*" or coerced homosexual partners; the 26s are associated with cunning, obtaining money and other goods by means of fraud and theft; the 27s protect and enforce the codes of the 28s and 26s, and are symbolized by blood. Other gangs, of more recent origin and regarded as illegitimate by the number gangs, are the Big Fives, who collaborate with the authorities as informers and in other ways; and the Air Force, who organize mass escapes. Minor local gangs, sometimes associated with gangs in the outside world, also exist. Gang membership is marked by tattoos, symbols and "uniforms" recognizable by all prisoners.[70]

Gang membership is theoretically voluntary, but the fact of confinement for up to twenty-three hours a day in overcrowded communal cells places enormous power in the hands of the gang hierarchies. Nevertheless, not all prisoners are gang members, though they may have to cooperate with the gangs in various ways.[71] During our visits to prisons, numerous prisoners expressed to us their desire to be free of the gang system and removed from the pressures inherent in sharing cramped quarters with groups founded on violent activity. This was especially true in Modderbee and Barberton prisons. On the other hand, gangs clearly provide a form of support structure to long-term prisoners deprived of any alternative means of socialization.

Gangs may deprive non-members of all their personal belongings or deny them access to privileges. Several ex-prisoners described to us the experience of arriving in the section for awaiting trial to have everything they had brought to prison taken away from them. One prisoner described having to "buy" the right to a bed from gang leaders in the cell. Another stated that he had been deprived of access to his visitors on

---

[70]Haysom, *Prison Gangs*; W.J. Schurink, "The world of the *Wetslaners*: an analysis of some organisational features in South African prisons," *Acta Criminologica*, Vol.2, No.2, 1989; Breyten Breytenbach *The True Confessions of an Albino Terrorist*, (New York: Farrar, Straus, & Giroux, 1983), pp. 272-278.

[71]Studies indicate gang membership of 50 to 90 percent in some institutions. Van Zyl Smit, *Prison Law and Practice*, p.49.

several occasions by gang leaders who had demanded payment to allow him to see them next time.

In theory, the number gangs are not antagonistic to each other, but in practice they are competing for scarce resources — including the recruitment of other prisoners. Accordingly, the potential for violent conflict is great. Each prison will tend to have one dominant gang, which imposes its own discipline beneath that of the prison authorities. Attempts to disturb this structure can lead to warfare between the gangs; large influxes of prisoners from other parts of the system may also upset an existing equilibrium. Approximately two weeks before we visited Kroonstad Medium A prison, a fight took place between the 26s and the Big Fives. Over 200 prisoners from the Cape area had recently been transferred to the prison, as a measure to relieve overcrowding. The newly arrived prisoners largely belonged to the 26s, and challenged the previous hegemony in the prison of the Big Fives. Four prisoners were seriously injured and treated in the hospital in the town, another six were treated in the prison hospital. In Barberton maximum prison, a fight involving the Big Fives, 26s and 28s had taken place in December 1992, two months before our visit. In August 1993, thirty-three prisoners at Leeuwkop maximum security prison were injured when rival gangs attacked each other and guards used birdshot to separate them. Three were hospitalized.[72] In October 1993, a wave of gang-related violence spread throughout a number of South African prisons, causing numerous injuries and some fatalities.

In addition to general conflict between two gangs, we received reports during our visits that gang-related assaults by prisoners on other prisoners were a daily occurrence in maximum security prisons, and common in all prisons. In Barberton maximum prison, a prisoner told us that he had been assaulted approximately one month before our visit by gangmembers. He spoke to us from a single cell, where he had been moved from a communal cell where he had been housed with prisoners from a different gang. Virtually all ex-prisoners that we interviewed

---

[72]*SA Conflict Monitor*, August 1993.

stated that they had witnessed, or themselves been subject to, gang-related assaults.[73]

Sexual assault between prisoners is also common and is bound up with the institutionalized system of "wyfies" within the 28 gang. An ex-prisoner from the main prison in Johannesburg known colloquially as "Sun City" for its floodlighting, described being assaulted by more than twenty prisoners who wanted to rape him one night soon after his arrival. He reported the assault to the warders, but gang members bribed the guard and he remained housed in the same cell for nine months. An ex-prisoner from Pollsmoor described sexual assault as "general and routine." Another ex-prisoner held in Groenpunt and Losperfontein prisons, who had joined the 28s as a teenager while in reformatory school, stated that rape of younger prisoners would happen "about every week."

In September 1992, a nineteen-year-old prisoner at Groenpunt prison in Vereeniging died in prison. Gerald Nkomo had complained to the authorities of being raped, and asked for a transfer to a different prison. A few days before he died, Nkomo's sister had visited him in prison, when he was in good health, but told her that he was scared that his cell mates were going to kill him because he was pressing his complaint of rape. In February 1993, after repeated requests from a prisoners' rights organization for an investigation, the Department of Correctional Services stated that the doctor who had examined Nkomo found no signs of rape, and that there would be no inquest into the death because Nkomo had died of "natural causes."[74]

The prison authorities acknowledge the existence of the gangs as a problem, and express their complete opposition to the gang system. Various methods are used to try to minimize gang activity, including housing members of different gangs in different communal cells (this was not the practice in all prisons we visited, but was the case, for example,

---

[73]Cases reaching the South African court system as a result of murders committed in prison confirm that gang members may be instructed to kill other prisoners. In such cases, the fact of gang membership may be regarded as extenuating circumstances. See, for example, *S. v. Masaku* 1985 3 SA 908 (A); *S. v. Magubane* 1987 2 SA 663 (A).

[74]Information supplied by NICRO-Johannesburg; see also, Jacquie Golding, "Warders blamed for prison killing," *Weekly Mail*, February 26 to March 4, 1993.

in Barberton maximum security prison), and punishment for activities connected with gang membership.[75] Prisoners may also request to be housed in single cells, and during our visits we spoke to several prisoners who were segregated in this way at their own request because they believed their lives to be in danger in the cell to which they had previously been assigned.

Nevertheless, it was clear to us from our interviews with prisoners and ex-prisoners that at least some prison warders are in active collaboration with the gang system. The very existence of a gang, the Big Five, whose stated aim is to collaborate with the authorities, is suggestive of a less than whole-hearted opposition to the gang system. Ex-prisoners, including members of the Big Five, described to us the system by which prisoners in the gang will collaborate with the authorities, participate in corrupt practices, or defend warders in court if they are accused of wrongdoing; in return they are granted early parole, good work assignments, and support against the other gangs.

Prisoners frequently labelled the Big Five gang as informers, and expressed their fear that their conversations with our representatives would be reported to the authorities by members of the gang who might be within earshot. At least two prisoners reported to us that attempts had been made on their lives by members of the Big Five acting on the instructions of warders to whom they had previously made complaints, and that the authorities had taken no action to protect them. One prisoner, held in solitary confinement in Barberton maximum security prison and facing a charge of murder, claimed that he had been caused to commit the murder by members of the prison staff. A recently released ex-prisoner who had been held in Modderbee and Leeuwkop, two of the most notorious prisons near Johannesburg, similarly claimed to have been a member of the Big Five and to have carried out a murder on the instructions of warders in the year before his release.

The causes of the gang system are complex, and difficult to address in the short term. It is clear, however, that the effects of the

---

[75]Departmental Orders provide that prison staff should pay immediate and thorough attention to requests from prisoners to sleep in a particular cell because their lives are threatened, and that certain categories of prisoners, including members of different gangs and informers to the police or prison staff, should be housed separately; DOB II(1)(g)(xii) and DOB II(3)(m)(vii). See also Van Zyl Smit, *Prison Law and Practice*, pp. 147 & 187.

system are multiplied by the lack of work or recreational activity, especially in maximum security prisons; the extreme overcrowding and consequent lack of privacy in many prisons; and the tolerance of elements within the prison authorities of some gang activities.

VII. POLICE LOCKUPS

PHYSICAL CONDITIONS

According to recent government statistics, at any given time, 12,000 pre-trial detainees are held in police lockups under the custody of the South African Police (SAP).[76] Under the law, a detainee may be held without charge, in a police lockup, for up to forty-eight hours, after which time he or she must be charged and brought before a magistrate and either released on bail or transported to a prison to await trial. Thereafter, the law states that unconvicted or convicted prisoners are to be detained in police lockups only if detention in a prison is not practicable, and in any event for not longer than a month, without the authority of the Commissioner.[77] A magistrate can extend the time a suspect awaiting trial is held in police custody. In practice, however, some prisoners spend as long as two months in these facilities.

We received different reports from different police officials as to how long detention in police cells might last in practice. In the Khayelitsha police lockup, a local police officer told us that the maximum length of time anyone was ever held at that station was six days. In the Verwoerdburg lockup, six youths, aged fifteen through seventeen, had a hearing before a magistrate on the day of our visit. At that hearing, their trial was postponed for three weeks and the magistrate ruled that they would await their day in court in the police lockup. In the Cape Town Central Police Station lockup we were told by the accompanying officers that a suspect could be held there for as long as four weeks.

Police lockups frequently also hold some sentenced prisoners, who are "loaned" to the police by the Correctional Services to provide a work force for the maintenance of the holding cells. Inmates sent to work at police stations are usually serving relatively short sentences or have just a few months left to serve and have a low security classification. Their stints in a lockup last between thirty and sixty days, according to various accounts given by police officials. Not all police lockups use prison labor; of those which use it, some bring prisoners in to work every day and take them back to prison in the evening.

---

[76]*Beeld*, September 3, 1992.

[77]Correctional Services Act, Section 28.

Police lockups, in theory, are meant for short-term stays only. As such, they provide very few amenities. With the exception of the Cape Town Central Police Station lockup, all lockups we saw were essentially similar. There were usually several communal cells and a few single cells. The communal cells usually held under ten detainees and consisted of two areas: the cell proper and an adjoining cement patio. A shower and a toilet were in the patio area. The cell usually had a cement bench as its only furniture. Prisoners slept on mats. There was a water fountain and a metal toilet in the cell. At night the cell was locked; during the day the door between the patio and the cell stayed open. Cells, when full to their stated capacity, were extremely crowded. For example, a six-person cell in Kensington measured 121 square feet, leaving slightly above twenty feet per prisoner. In facts, since some of the space was taken up by a toilet and most of the space by the sleeping mats, there was very little room to move around in the cell. In Khayelitsha, a cell with capacity for twenty-four measured 364 square feet, affording about fifteen square feet per prisoner. Since a sleeping mat takes up at least twelve feet, there was hardly any space left when the cell was full.

The Cape Town lockup, located downtown in a large city building, had an entirely different layout and no patios adjoining the cells. There was a larger cement patio in the center of the cell area. The cell block consisted of cells of various sizes, not all of which had windows.

All police cells we visited were poorly lit and had bad ventilation. We were told that the cells were not warm enough at night and could get very hot during the day.

All cells were closed at night, and the door was usually solid metal. There were no devices such as buzzers to summon guards in the case of an emergency. We were told that prisoners would yell if they needed to summon a guard. In the Cape Town lockup that system seemed particularly problematic. The largest cell was located the farthest away from the guard station and was separated from it by a two-inch thick solid metal door, and an approximately forty-step corridor with a bend. It seemed very unlikely that a guard could hear anybody calling for help. In all lockups, we were told that during the night guards walked through the cells every thirty minutes or every hour for security reasons.

VIOLENCE

South African police stations have a reputation for extreme violence. Reports indicate that detainees are often tortured, sometimes as acts of random violence meant as intimidation or as a means of summary justice, but most often to extract confessions. Local human rights organizations attempting to assist victims in bringing actions for damages against the police report that assaults in police custody are routine and brutal.

A police spokesman told us in an interview that a police officer can take a confession but that "its validity will be tested in court." To invalidate such a confession we were told that the suspect has to prove that undue influence was used to obtain the confession.[78] In a report on the conduct of the police in their investigation of the "Boipatong massacre" in which forty-two township residents were killed in June 1992, British criminologist Dr. Peter Waddington concluded that allegations of torture by the police gave rise to the well-founded "suspicion that the style of investigation adopted in this case, and perhaps in South Africa generally, is *confession oriented*."[79] The report stated that unlawful means for the extraction of confessions would be likely as a result of the failure of the police, described in the report, to use other methods of investigation.

Under the Inquest Act, in the case of an unnatural death where there is not enough evidence to charge anyone immediately, an autopsy must be conducted to try to establish the cause of death, and an inquest is compulsory. However, autopsies are carried out by a state pathologist or district surgeon, both of whom are state employees, and most inquests are held informally. The family of the deceased usually has no legal representation, and no witnesses are called or cross-examined. In these circumstances a magistrate has little option but to accept the police version of events. The family of a person who died in police custody may now appoint an independent pathologist to be present during the autopsy; but the autopsy is carried out at a state mortuary, and there is no requirement to wait for the family's representative: 90 percent of

---

[78] Interview with Col. Frank Alton, Pretoria, August 18, 1992.

[79] Dr. P.A.J. Waddington, Director, Criminal Justice Studies, University of Reading, England, *Report of the Inquiry into the Police Response to and Investigation of Events in Boipatong on 17 June 1992*; Submitted to the Commission of Inquiry regarding the Prevention of Public Violence and Intimidation, July 20, 1992; pp. 41-42.

inquests take place without the presence of a private medical practitioner appointed by the family.[80]

The issue of violence in police custody became the focus of media and political attention in July 1992, when one of the country's most prominent physicians, the independent pathologist Dr. Jonathan Gluckman, opened his files to a reporter and stated that police were responsible for 90 percent of the 200 deaths he investigated in his career. Dr. Gluckman first won an international reputation for his evidence in the 1977 inquest into the death in police custody of the black activist Steve Biko. The case that Gluckman said was the last straw was the July 1992 death of nineteen-year old Simon Mthimkulu of the township of Sebokeng. Gluckman was quoted in *The New York Times* as saying "This is a 19-year-old boy.... Not charged with any offense. Tortured, ill-treated and killed. He could have been a son of mine."[81]

Dr. Gluckman's files span several years, and it is impossible to assess the frequency of death in custody based on these alone. He himself pointed out that he only examined bodies when retained by legal representatives of the family of the deceased. In almost all the cases, the victims are black and poor: it is safe to assume that most of their relatives do not have the means to retain legal advisers or independent pathologists. Furthermore, not all of those with such means would have retained Dr. Gluckman as their medical examiner during the period of which he was speaking. The numbers are therefore likely to be significantly higher than those he quoted.

Based on police data, an average of more than two deaths a week occurred in police custody during the eighteen months preceding Dr. Gluckman's revelations. The chart below shows the official reasons given for each of these deaths.[82]

---

[80]Loraine Gordon, "Independent forensic service can monitor police actions," *Weekly Mail and Guardian*, Review Law Supplement, (Johannesburg), September 1993.

[81]Bill Keller, "South Africa Police Said to Kill Captives," *The New York Times*, July 27, 1992.

[82]Interview with Col. Frank Alton, Pretoria, August 18, 1992.

January 1, 1991 - June 30, 1992
deaths in detention
(with the exclusion of shootouts in pursuit)

natural causes	31
suicides	49
attempted escape	14
self-defense by police	4
pre-existing condition	20
assaulted by members of the public before apprehension	27
assaulted by inmates	7
deaths in detention when members of police prosecuted	6
still under investigation, with a possibility of prosecution	12
TOTAL	170

But the number of deaths in police custody may even be higher. Based on press reports, at least six people died in police custody in the two weeks immediately after Dr. Gluckman's statement, and twenty died in less than two months following his revelations.[83] According to the Human Rights Commission, an independent Johannesburg-based monitoring organization, 123 people died in police custody in 1992, and thirty-five during the first ten months of 1993. According to the Minister of Law and Order, 114 people died in police custody in 1992: twenty-one of natural causes, fifty-three by suicide, twelve from injuries sustained before arrest, and twenty-eight from "other causes."[84]

In the aftermath of Dr. Gluckman's account, and the release of the Waddington report, the police took certain measures aimed at investigating the allegations. A number of high ranking officers were dismissed, and a commission of six magistrates was established to investigate the allegations of torture in police lockups. In November 1992, it was announced that twelve retired magistrates had in fact been appointed to prevent and investigate deaths in police custody, and that an additional twenty former police generals had been appointed to visit

---

[83]The Associated Press, September 23, 1992.

[84]Human Rights Commission "Human Rights Review 1992 (Johannesburg);" Minister of Law and Order quoted in *SA Conflict Monitor*, March 1993.

police cells. More significantly, in October 1992 the International Committee of the Red Cross was given access to South African police stations for the first time. In January 1993, the police cited Red Cross advice in an announcement that R.12 million ($4 million) would be spent on upgrading police cells. At the same time as these steps were taken, however, a campaign to discredit Dr. Gluckman was launched. In November 1992, it was discovered that Dr. Gluckman's office in downtown Johannesburg was bugged and that his phone was tapped.[85]

In December 1992 the results of an investigation into 118 cases described by Dr. Gluckman were published by the Minister of Law and Order, Hernus Kriel. The minister stated that only thirty-four of those listed by Dr. Gluckman had in fact died in police custody. Dr. Gluckman rejected the report as inadequate to deal with his allegations. Although it had been reported that this report was only part of a much wider investigation into all deaths in police custody over the previous two years, a spokesperson for the minister said in February 1993 that "the intention was never to conduct an in-depth investigation into every case."[86] Gluckman died in May 1993, before completing his exposé of police brutality towards detainees.[87]

Inquests must be held after any death in police custody, though in most cases they are conducted by a magistrate on the basis only of evidence submitted by the police themselves. In some circumstances, usually where the family of the deceased has obtained legal representation and alternative evidence is presented, these inquests confirm police responsibility. For example, in March 1993 an inquest into the death of Bethuel Maphumulo in police custody in December 1990 concluded that Maphumulo had been strangled to death by a police lieutenant. The lieutenant concerned was suspended from duty by the SAP only after an outcry at the force's initial refusal to do so. Even when a formal inquest with full legal representation is announced, however, the cause of death may be difficult to determine as a result of delay and

---

[85] David Beresford, "Bugs at office of SA pathologist in police death row," *The Guardian* (London), November 11, 1992.

[86] *Saturday Star*, (Johannesburg) February 20, 1993.

[87] Human Rights Watch spoke to Dr. Gluckman in South Africa before his death.

obstruction to the carrying-out of an investigation. In June 1993, an inquest decided that it was unable to determine the cause of death of Nickson Phiri, who died in the notorious Welverdiend police station in January 1990.[88]

Even in very controversial cases, a formal inquest is not always held. On July 10, 1993, Victor Kheswa, known as the "Vaal Monster" for his alleged involvement in a number of mass murders in townships near Johannesburg, died in police custody. Kheswa was revealed after his death to have been a member both of the Inkatha Freedom Party (IFP) and of the extreme right-wing World Preservatist Movement, and allegations were immediately made that he had been killed to stop him confirming right-wing involvement in political violence if he were tried. A special investigation led by high-level police officers was announced on July 14; the next day the head of the investigation announced that he was "completely happy that Kheswa was not assaulted by the police." On July 30, it was reported that the results of the postmortem showed that Kheswa died of natural causes; however, an independent postmortem, conducted by a doctor commissioned by Kheswa's family and the IFP, found that Kheswa died of unnatural causes, possibly from "acute suffocation, electrocution and hypothermia, as well as occult toxic substances." Despite this finding, it was announced in late August that no formal inquest would be held, based on the conclusion of the state pathologist.[89]

The security forces of the ten "homelands" in South Africa, created as part of the apartheid system to give black South Africans citizenship in nominally independent states and deprive them of their rights as South African citizens, are particularly notorious for their abuses of detainees. The police force in KwaZulu, the political base of Chief Gatsha Buthelezi, President of the Inkatha Freedom Party and Chief Minister of the homeland, has been exposed on numerous occasions for

---

[88]For background on the Welverdiend police station, see Africa Watch, *Half-Hearted Reform: The official response to the rising tide of violence* (New York: Human Rights Watch, May 1993), pp. 49 & 51.

[89]Human Rights Commission, *Monthly Repression Reports*, July and August 1993.

its brutality and violence.[90] In Bophuthatswana, in a series of egregious incidents in 1993, police repeatedly detained and assaulted student leaders on the campus of the University of Bophuthatswana in Mmabatho.

In January 1993, South Africa signed the Convention against Torture and Other Cruel, Inhuman or Degrading Treatment or Punishment.[91] In July 1993 the Security Forces Board of Inquiry Act provided for a judge of the Supreme Court to inquire into serious offenses committed by members of the police and other security forces. In addition, procedures were instituted under the National Peace Accord during 1993 for lay visiting of police cells in most urban areas.[92]

Despite these measures taken to increase supervision of police detention, allegations of ill-treatment in police custody continued during 1993, and the great majority of police alleged to be responsible for abuse of detainees were not held accountable for their actions. In July, Advocate Jan Munnik, Police Reporting Officer for the Witwatersrand, reported use of torture by a special unit of the police known as the "Yankee

---

[90]See *"Traditional Dictatorship": One Party State in KwaZulu Homeland Threatens Transition to Democracy*, News from Africa Watch, Vol.5, No.12, September 1993. In December 1993, the Commission of Inquiry Regarding the Prevention of Public Violence and Intimidation, chaired by Mr. Justice Richard Goldstone, confirmed that members of the KZP trained by the South African army in Namibia's Caprivi strip during the 1980s had been operating as hit squads in KwaZulu.

[91]Though South Africa has not yet ratified the convention, and is not therefore bound by its more detailed provisions, the prohibition on torture is part of international customary law, by which South Africa is bound. Article 5 of the Universal Declaration of Human Rights (UDHR) also prohibits torture, or cruel, inhuman or degrading treatment or punishment. The UDHR is regarded as the authoritative interpretation of the human rights obligations of member states of the United Nations, of which South Africa is one.

[92]The National Peace Accord is a wide-ranging agreement signed in September 1991 by a number of political and other organizations with the aim of reducing political violence in South Africa.

Squad."[93] Torture methods included electric shocks, heads being held under water, and death threats. In the wake of the investigation the unit was disbanded, but similar allegations continued to be made of other units, both within the SAP and within other security forces, including the independently commanded police forces of the black homelands.

As in the case of prison warders, civil actions for damages based on assault are hindered by a six-month limitation period within which a case must be commenced.[94] Public interest lawyers attempting to bring cases based on allegations of police brutality repeatedly find that their clients, attempting to report an assault, have been put off by the police until after the six-month period has expired.

---

[93] Police Reporting Officers for ten districts covering all South Africa were appointed in January 1993, under the terms of the National Peace Accord of September 1991. The reporting officers have the responsibility to investigate police misconduct.

[94] Police Act 1958, Section 32; as in the Correctional Services Act, one month's notice must also be given to the defendant, reducing the period to an effective five months.

VIII. CONTACTS WITH THE OUTSIDE

As described earlier, South African prisons were for years surrounded by a veil of secrecy. The press was severely restricted in writing about prison matters, and in practice hardly ever covered prison stories for fear of costly lawsuits. Writing about prison experience even in a private letter was illegal.

The recent changes in the law have improved the situation with respect to the media and publishing. But conveying information about prison conditions in the course of a private conversation between an inmate and a visitor, for example, may still be considered a violation of prison rules. During our 1993 visit to the Brandvlei prison, we saw a sign in the visiting area that listed rules for visits. Item number 2 provided: "No discussions on prison administrations [sic] will be allowed."

VISITS

As described in the sections regarding the classification groups, contact with the outside depends to a large extent on the "privilege group" under which a particular inmate has been classified.[95]

Only prisoners with the highest "privilege" classification, group A, are entitled to contact visits. Unsentenced prisoners do not have contact visits regardless of the charge or the length of their pre-trial detention, though the number of visits they may receive is unlimited. Sentenced or unsentenced prisoners held in police lockups may in practice receive a limited number of visits, whatever their theoretical entitlement. Police lockups have no facilities for visits (since they are not supposed to hold anybody for longer than forty-eight hours), and visits may be limited only to weekends, as was the case in Verwoerdburg, for example.

The frequency and duration of visits and the number of persons allowed to visit also depend on the classification. Group D can have up to twelve visits a year; group C twenty-four visits; group B thirty-six visits; and group A forty-eight visits. For all groups, the visits need to be evenly spaced in time. Only one person can visit a group D prisoner at a time; prisoners classified as C and B can be visited by up to two persons at a

---

[95]Rule 37 of the U.N. Standard Minimum Rules provides that "Prisoners shall be allowed under necessary supervision to communicate with their family and reputable friends at regular intervals, both by correspondence and by receiving visits."

time; and for group A the number of visitors is to be determined by the head of the prison. Children under the age of sixteen do not count as visitors, and their admission is subject to the suitability of the visiting facilities. A single visit for groups D through B can last up to thirty minutes; for group A the duration is up to forty minutes.

Non-contact visits are conducted in specially designed booths. A row of, say, twenty prisoners may sit on stools on one side of a glass or plastic screen, with partitions separating each prisoner from the next. Facing them, through the screen, is another stool (one only) for the visitor to sit at, again separated by a partition from the next visitor. The partitions are not sufficient to soundproof each booth from the next. An intercom system, operated by buttons pushed by the person speaking, allows communication between the two sides of the screen. A warder supervising the visits may listen to the conversations through the use of an extra receiver on the inmate's side of the partition. Where there is no intercom, as for example in Pretoria, inmates are supervised by guards who walk up and down the room.

Contact visits are conducted in general visiting areas, under guards' supervision. Those we saw varied from gloomy hallways to relatively pleasant outdoor courtyards. In at least one case, we heard a complaint from an ex-prisoner who had group A classification that when no guard was available to supervise, he would get visits through the glass partition, even though he was entitled to contact visits. In Modderbee prison we received reports that relatives had to bribe staff members in order to be able to visit prisoners.

Contacts between inmates and their relatives are severely limited by the fact that many prisoners are held in institutions far away from their area of residence. It puts a heavy burden on relatives to undertake a lengthy trip to a distant area in order to be able to see an inmate for just thirty minutes. Even when prisoners are held in institutions near their home town, getting to the prison is not always easy. The Pollsmoor prisons, although only a few miles out of town, are accessible only by car and thus difficult to reach for most visitors. Robben Island, meanwhile, can be reached only by boat. Visitors must make arrangements with the Department of Correctional Services several days in advance to be able to get to the prison. The rules allow the head of a prison to permit several visits to be combined into one of longer duration, or to have several visits within just a few days; and at the time of our visit to the Westville complex in Durban, prisoners were allowed to combine two thirty-minute visits into one. However, this relaxation of the rules is at the discretion of each prison head, and is not the case at all prisons.

CORRESPONDENCE

According to prison officials, for two years now, prisoners have been able to send and receive an unlimited number of letters. Prison officials may check the letters in either direction.

But at Brandvlei, for example, we were told by inmates that letters had to be authorized by the head of the prison and that there were some problems with mail delivery. We heard similar complaints from prisoners at Barberton, who alleged that the officers mailed the letters out selectively. At Barberton in particular, but also in other prisons, inmates also complained that they had difficulty contacting lawyers or prisoners' aid organizations.

USE OF THE TELEPHONE

For a few years now, prisoners in South Africa have been allowed to make a limited number of telephone calls. Prisoners may make a phone call *instead* of a visit, and only on weekends and public holidays. Group D prisoners may not make any phone calls; group A prisoners are allowed to make an extra twelve phone calls per year, in addition to those they might want to substitute for visits. Each phone call may last up to ten minutes. Phones are not available in all the prisons. For example, in the Durban Westville complex, the male prisons had them but the only female prison did not.

ACCESS TO NEWS

In the past, all access to news, especially for political prisoners, was strictly controlled. Currently, the degree to which an inmate can keep abreast with developments on the outside depends chiefly on his or her classification group and financial situation. Complete isolation from developments in the outside world is no longer inflicted on any prisoner. Inmates with D classification are not allowed access to news. The other groups, to which most prisoners belong, are allowed to purchase newspapers and magazines and the amounts spent do not count toward the overall limit on spending money. Inmates classified A can own a TV set in their cells. In some prisons, inmates in lower groups can collectively rent or purchase a TV, and many prisoners have radios.

Access to legal advice

The Correctional Services Act and Regulations provide that a prisoner may have access to legal advice in connection with criminal proceedings or a civil action, subject to the permission of the Commissioner and any conditions set by the Commissioner.[96] The right of access to legal counsel as part of the right of access to the courts was recognized in the leading case of *Mandela v. Minister of Prisons*.[97] Interviews must be conducted within sight, though not hearing, of a member of the prison staff. Sound recording equipment may not be used, and a prisoner may not hand any document to his or her lawyer without the permission of the authorities. Right to legal representation at a disciplinary hearing before an institutional committee is specifically excluded by the Act, although a lawyer may be retained if the hearing is before a magistrate.[98]

The economic realities of South Africa mean that the vast majority of prisoners have no lawyer, and were convicted or are held in custody pending trial without ever having received legal assistance. Many prisoners do attempt to contact groups that provide free advice, such as Lawyers for Human Rights, the National Institute for Crime Prevention and the Rehabilitation of Offenders (NICRO), or the Legal Resources Centre. These letters are generally smuggled out of the prison: several prisoners complained to us that letters to lawyers complaining about prison conditions were confiscated or censored; others requested that no reply should be sent, or the prisoner would be punished. South African prisons do not have law libraries enabling prisoners to consult texts on their rights.

Groups dealing with prisoners' rights who wish to take action on the basis of letters that they receive are hampered by lack of resources to handle the number of requests for assistance. The physical remoteness of many of the prisons from large population centers means that it is a major investment of time and money to visit a single prisoner in one of these prisons. Lawyers are additionally restricted by the fact that only qualified attorneys are automatically allowed to consult with prisoners to

---

[96] Correctional Services Regulations, Regulation 123.

[97] 1983 1 SA 938 (A); however, the case upheld the right of the state to restrict a prisoner's rights to pass written material to his lawyer.

[98] Correctional Services Act, Sections 51(3) and 54(10).

give legal advice; paralegals or trainee attorneys do not generally have visiting rights. Although groups such as Lawyers for Human Rights have made special arrangements with the Department of Correctional Services for their paralegals to be able to visit prisoners, removal of this restriction would allow more prisoners to get legal assistance. In addition, a lawyer may not request to see a prisoner on the basis of information received through unofficial channels, nor discuss the prisoner's legal concerns in general, but must have an official request from that prisoner or a member of his or her family in order to obtain permission to visit from the authorities. In theory, a prisoner may only discuss ongoing or proposed litigation during a lawyer's visit, and may not discuss his or her general legal rights under prison law. In practice, however, this last provision no longer appears to be applied.

 Judges and magistrates have the right to visit prisons at any time.[99] Although potentially a powerful tool to correct complaints at prison conditions, it appears that this power is irregularly used and of little effect in practice. The only mechanism explicitly provided in the regulations is for the judicial officer to report matters of concern to the Commissioner of Prisons.[100]

---

[99] Correctional Services Regulations, Regulation 104(2); a judge may visit any prison in South Africa, a magistrate any prison within his jurisdiction.

[100] See also, Van Zyl Smit, *Prison Law and Practice*, pp. 168 & 247.

IX. WORK

Prison labor has historically played an important role in the country's economy. In the nineteenth century, prisoners built roads and all the major mountain passes. Unskilled prison labor was used in gold and diamond mining. After the 1950s, with the abolition of the sentence of hard labor, prisoners were no longer used for mining, but they continued to be hired out to the private sector, especially agriculture. Under a variety of arrangements, farmers were able to hire prison labor cheaply. For example, a network of prison farm outstations was built by groups of farmers and handed over to the authorities, who kept these institutions stocked with prisoners. Farmers paid very reduced fees for the labor thus obtained. In addition, a system of "parole" into the farms existed for short-term prisoners. These systems were sources of strong criticism from South Africa's trading partners as well as from the human rights community.[101] South Africa was repeatedly accused of slavery by means of its prison system. The extent of the problem can be illustrated by a case of a farmer from northern Transvaal, accused of beating his naked "parole" prisoners. At his hearing he testified that between 1972 and 1977, no fewer than 4,000 prisoners worked on his farm.[102]

Under pressure from the international community on human rights grounds, and on the grounds that the outstation system violated the General Agreement on Tariffs and Trade (GATT), South Africa dismantled the system allowing the hire of prison labor by the private sector in the late 1980s. However, prisoners are still released on "parole" to work in private sector businesses, where they may receive little or no remuneration. Prisoners' rights activists stated to us that the system still allowed abuse.

Within the prison system itself, prisoners have for a long period been employed on prison-owned farms. In the past, the prison system has also employed inmates in various forms of hard labor, including stonework. For example, political prisoners on Robben Island worked

---

[101]Dirk Van Zyl Smit, "South Africa," in Van Zyl Smit and Dünkel (eds.), *Imprisonment Today and Tomorrow*, p. 549.

[102]Mihálik, "Restrictions on Prison Reporting" p.408.

mainly in quarries. A particularly notorious place was the quarry in Barberton, where prisoners from privilege group D worked in cages, meant to prevent them from assaulting each other. On December 29, 1982, several prisoners died there, allegedly of heat prostration. The quarry no longer exists.

Prisons are supposed to be self-sufficient. In 1991, amendments to prison legislation introduced a new policy of running the prison system on business principles. A White Paper issued by the Departments of Justice and Correctional Services, on which the amendments were based, stated, in the section titled "Economizing of the Department of Correctional Services," "The goal of this strategy is to strive towards the optimization of resources in order to bring about greater cost-effectiveness, to optimize self-sufficiency and to generate income for own requirements."[103]

Despite their abusive history and recent commitment to commercialization, South African prisons have had a theoretical commitment to the rehabilitative character of prison labor, almost since they were established. Since 1959, the functions of the prison service have been stated to include the duty "so far as practicable, to apply such treatment to convicted prisoners ... as may lead to their reformation and rehabilitation and to train them in habits of industry and labour."[104] The aim of the "treatment and training" is to equip the prisoner for, and to cultivate a desire to, lead "an honest and industrious life" after his or her release; and "to develop self-respect and a sense of responsibility."[105] Most prisoners and ex-prisoners that we spoke to had absorbed to a striking extent the idea that prison should rehabilitate them for return to a non-criminal life outside the prison; but most also expressed extreme discontent with the work and training actually available to them while in prison.

---

[103] Republic of South Africa, Departments of Justice and Correctional Services, "White Paper on the Extension of the Mission of the Department of Correctional Services and the Implementation of Correctional Supervision as an Alternative Sentencing Option," 6 May 1991.

[104] Correctional Services Act, Section 2(2)(b).

[105] Correctional Services Regulations, Regulation 117(1).

South African prisoners, with the exception of pre-trial detainees, are theoretically obliged to work, although employment is not in fact available to all prisoners.[106] Refusal to work is a disciplinary infraction, though a medical officer must certify that a prisoner is fit to work and has the power to exempt a prisoner from working.[107] Most prisoners are not paid for their labor, though some in more skilled employment may receive a small gratuity, amounting to the equivalent of a few dollars a month. In several prisons, prisoners complained to us that they were exploited and made to work too hard. Several prisoners and ex-prisoners alleged that they had been forced to work while they were ill.

Medium security male prisoners may be employed as agricultural laborers on farms belonging to the Correctional Services, which produce products mostly for use within the prison system; elsewhere, they may work as cleaners, gardeners, or maintenance staff on or off the prison premises. Prisoners also work in construction and repair of prison facilities and prison staff housing (many white staff members live on prison grounds); those with the necessary skills may work on repairing cars or machinery belonging to the prison system or other government agencies.

Prisoners in maximum security prisons (about 15 percent of the prison population[108]) usually do not work, and may as a consequence be confined to their cells for all but a half-hour- or hour-long exercise period a day. Many prisoners in maximum security institutions complained to us about their inactivity and boredom, often stating that violence and gang activity in the prison were made worse by the lack of other occupation, or that the lack of work would make them unemployable once they were released. In Brandvlei maximum security prison, while some prisoners did work on some days, they complained that the work consisted only of chopping wood.

---

[106]Section 77 of the Correctional Services Act states that "Every prisoner ... shall at all times perform such labour, tasks and other duties as may be assigned to him...."

[107]Correctional Services Regulations, Regulations 99(1)(d) and 105(2).

[108]Report for the Period 1, July 1990-30 June 1991, Department of Correctional Services, Republic of South Africa.

Female prisoners are usually employed in laundry and sewing activities. For example, in the Durban prison, women did the laundry not only for their own facility but also for the four male prisons and the staff. In Kroonstad, women were sewing mattress covers, pajamas, and their own uniforms; others did the laundry for the whole prison. The women in prison in Umtata, Transkei, were also responsible for laundry for both men's and women's prisons.

Some short-term prisoners with low security classifications are also employed in police stations, generally in the maintenance of police lockups. They are transferred daily to stations located near prisons, or may live for as long as two months in the police lockup itself. They may also be used in the maintenance of court rooms, or in similar tasks within the justice system.

Vocational training is available to a small proportion of prisoners and almost exclusively to the male inmates. According to prison officials, an inmate has to be serving a sentence of at least four years' imprisonment in order to be eligible for vocational training. As of June 30, 1991, a total of 2,581 prisoners were receiving vocational training, nine of them were women.[109] About 3 percent of the prison population was therefore receiving vocational training at that time. Trade tests confirming that an individual has received training are available to the prisoners in theory, though some prisoners complained about access to these tests in practice.

According to officials in Kroonstad, until racial integration began to be implemented, only whites had access to the impressive set of workshops providing vocational training in the Medium B prison. Even though this training is now nominally available to all races, during our visit we saw predominantly white prisoners in the workshops, even though whites constituted a fraction of the overall population of the prison complex. In other prisons, workshops were usually small in size, sufficient only to supply the needs of the prison rather than to provide training for a significant number of prisoners. Some prisoners were, however, being trained in these workshops; an apparently disproportionate number of these prisoners were white.

---

[109] *Ibid.*

Vocational training for women at Kroonstad was limited to hairdressing, and they did not have access to the impressive workshops available to the men.

Prisoners who enter prison already qualified in some way — as plumbers, carpenters, electricians, and so forth — are likely to be employed within the prison system. As such, they do not receive further training, but they are paid a nominal fee for their work, and may receive a certificate on release confirming their employment in that capacity.

X. ACTIVITIES

Idleness and boredom were among the most frequently voiced complaints during our prison visits. Even where prisoners work, cells were usually locked for the night at about 4:00 P.M. and opened before breakfast the next morning. Prisoners who did not work often spent the entire day locked up in their severely overcrowded cells, except for short periods of exercise. In either case, there is very little with which to fill the time.

RECREATION

In the prisons visited by Human Rights Watch, most prisoners had access to some sort of physical recreation, but often as seldom as once a week. In Barberton, prisoners in one section reported that they had been forbidden sports activities for three months, as a form of collective punishment, and alleged that the volleyball game that we witnessed took place specifically because of our February 17, 1993 visit. They said that the last time they had been allowed sports was in November 1992.

An ex-prisoner recently released from Modderbee reported that the only recreational activity prisoners in his section of the prison had access to were soccer games on Sundays. As in Barberton, these might be cancelled if anyone in the section committed a disciplinary infraction. Some of the prisoners interviewed at Modderbee prison reported that they were allowed only an average of two to three hours outdoors a week. They also pointed out that it was because of our visit that they were authorized to exercise on that day. Barberton prison is famous for its boxing, and tournaments are arranged between the different prisons in the complex, sometimes in public. Prisoners generally complained to us about the poor quality of sports equipment, and that they had to pay for items such as balls.

Prisoners in groups A, B and C are allowed to have their own private radios, and group A inmates are allowed televisions, though they have to buy the TV sets or pay for the rental themselves. In some cases, prisoners complained that there were no plugs in their cells and therefore electrical appliances could not be used. Movies, selected by the prison staff or recreation committee (consisting of prisoner representatives), are shown at intervals in many of the prisons.

Only sentenced prisoners have access to prison libraries. These libraries are stocked from local libraries, and the books are exchanged regularly. However, several prisoners complained to us at the quality of the selection of books available to them. Libraries do not include law books for prisoners to use to research their own cases. The right to purchase newspapers and magazines is theoretically limited by privilege group, but these restrictions seemed to be breaking down at those prisons we visited. Evidently, access to broadcast news services has rendered this aspect of censorship meaningless. Unsentenced inmates are allowed, according to the regulations, to purchase magazines and newspapers.

Only prisoners of the two highest classification categories are allowed to practice hobbies, such as crafts. Prisoners in the highest, A group, may be allowed to have pets. We observed one prisoner, a "monitor," with a cat as a pet, which he was allowed to keep in his dormitory cell; we also saw caged birds as pets in various cells.

Female prisoners also had access to some sports, usually netball (a sport usually played by women that is similar to basketball) or volleyball. However, as was the case for work opportunities, much recreational activity for women was stereotypically "feminine," including jewelry classes and fashion shows.

EDUCATION

Prisoners may study. Part of the stated purpose of imprisonment is to provide "treatment and training," and thus education is officially encouraged if "a prisoner's deficient or inadequate schooling ... could possibly be a factor in causing crime." However, the regulation dealing with education provides that "Permission to study ... is subject to the discretion of the Commissioner and [the regulation] may in no way be construed as implying that [it] allows any prisoner a right which he can legally claim."[110]

At the most basic literacy level, a prison usually organizes classes and provides educational materials. These classes are taught by other prisoners, who are paid a nominal fee for this work. Trained teachers are

---

[110] Correctional Services Regulations, Regulation 109(1) & (6).

not provided.[111] At higher levels, prisoners may take correspondence courses, but they have to pay the tuition and buy all the books, which they may receive by mail. We spoke to many prisoners who were studying by correspondence, including a handful at degree level; however, many more inmates expressed an interest in studying at higher levels and sorrow because they could not afford the cost.

A nineteen-year-old at the Modderbee prison told us that he had completed the basic education in prison and wanted to continue to the next level. "They sent me papers saying that education is not a right but a privilege. My parents don't live in this area, and so I don't have any money."

---

[111] According to the Department of Correctional Services, those prisoners who are selected to teach classes operate under the supervision of a trained instructor, who is a member of the Department. At higher primary school levels, classes are taught by trained instructors or qualified teachers, and at levels up to Matric (the highschool leaving exam) by qualified teachers.

XI. SPECIAL CATEGORIES OF PRISONERS

WOMEN

As in most countries, women form a small proportion of the prison population in South Africa. On December 31, 1992, there were 3,369 female prisoners (790 of them unsentenced), accounting for 3 percent of the general prison population.[112] As a consequence, women are not subject to the same conditions of overcrowding as male prisoners.

In the Durban Westville and Pollsmoor prisons, which formerly held black prisoners, female inmates were housed in communal cells similar to those for men, though in substantially less crowded conditions. Some women were held in much smaller cells holding four or six inmates each, and some lived in single cells. In Kroonstad women's prison, which formerly held only white prisoners, almost all women — black and white — were kept in single cells, decorated by their occupants, whose individual doors were never locked. As is common in prisons worldwide, the atmosphere in women's prisons generally was much less harsh than in those housing men.

The flip side of this situation is that there are fewer institutions holding women (in recent years, the number of institutions or sections of prisons holding women has been reduced to accommodate the faster-growing male population) and consequently, women tend to be held in prisons further away from their homes than men. They have fewer visits as a result.

Another visits-related problem particularly serious for women with young children is the fact that only prisoners with group A classification are entitled to contact visits. As explained in the chapter on the "privilege" system, it takes approximately a year to reach group A from the moment of entering the prison, regardless of the crime committed, the sentence imposed and the security assessment. This means that thousands of children of female prisoners are denied the right to

---

[112]Based on data provided in an April 2, 1993 letter to Human Rights Watch from the Department of Correctional Services.

have any physical contact with their mothers.[113] In fact, relatively few women ever reach group A, because their sentences tend to be shorter and they simply do not stay in prison long enough to go from the entry C level all the way to A. For example, out of the 495 women in the Durban prison on the day of our visit, eighty-five were classified in group A. In Pretoria, of the eighty-seven female inmates, only two were group A prisoners. In Pollsmoor, of the 340 female inmates on the day of our visit, only twenty-six had group A classification. Only women who commit more serious crimes stand a chance of eventually being able to have contact visits of any sort. This practice, in addition to affecting the inmates, victimizes the children, who suffer from lack of physical contact with their mothers.

The South African prison system allows women with children of up to two years of age, and in some cases up to four years, to keep the children with them in prison. As of May 1993, there were 189 children under four years of age in the prisons.[114] In prisons we visited, there were limited special arrangements for mothers and children. Cribs were located in regular cells, next to the mothers' beds, so that mother and child could be together at night. If the mothers were required to work, their babies were cared for during the mothers' work hours in moderately well-appointed nurseries by assigned prisoners. Babies born in prison do not have that fact noted on their birth registration document.

Women are at a disadvantage compared with their male counterparts in prisons in several other areas. Where there is work, they are usually required to perform what one prison official accompanying our representatives described as "typically women's work," such as laundry or sewing. There is hardly any vocational training for women. According to government statistics, as of June 30, 1991, out of 2,581 prisoners receiving vocational training nationwide, only nine were female. They

---

[113] According to the Department of Correctional Services, in cases where a mother does not qualify for a contact visit under her privilege classification, "consultation visits" at which contact is allowed may be granted by the head of the prison. However, such a visit is at the discretion of the officer, if he regards it to be in the interest of the mother or the child, and is not a matter of right.

[114] Moses Mamaila and Justice Mohale, "The Cell Block Kids," *City Press*, (Johannesburg) May 23, 1993.

Prison Conditions in South Africa 73

were training as hairdressers. In one prison complex, in Durban, the female prison was the only institution without phones for inmates' use.

JUVENILES

Age	Number of prisoners
7-13	18
14	50
15	122
16	377
17	879
18	3,614
19	4,227
20	4,903
21	2,269
Total	16,459

One of the striking features in South African prisons is the presence of very young prisoners. During our visit to the Pollsmoor Maximum Security prison, we saw inmates as young as ten years of age. At the time of our visit, Sections E1 and E2 of that prison held over 200 juvenile prisoners each: one section held those already sentenced; the other, children awaiting trial.

The chart above, based on official statistics, shows the numbers of juveniles of different age groups (sentenced and unsentenced) held in prisons as of December 31, 1992.[115] South African prison law classifies as juveniles persons under twenty-one years of age. These figures do not include juveniles held in police lockups.

Of the total, 5,208 were awaiting trial, of whom 720 were under eighteen years of age. Of all the juveniles being held in prison, 1,446

---

[115] April 2, 1993 letter from Correctional Services to Human Rights Watch.

were under eighteen; in November 1992, this figure had been 2,656.[116]

Under the Child Care Act of 1973, unconvicted children who are awaiting trial are supposed to be held in a designated "place of safety." They are not to be held in police cells unless their detention is "necessary" and "no suitable place of safety ... is available."[117] However, there are insufficient "places of safety" available to hold all the children in custody awaiting trial. In addition, police make inadequate efforts to trace children's parents or guardians in order to release the children into their parents' care. Many hundreds of children are therefore held in police cells unnecessarily, often for periods of weeks at a time.[118] In May 1992, the Minister of Law and Order stated to Parliament that 595 children under eighteen were being held awaiting trial in police cells on December

---

[116] Scott Kraft, "Jail Torment for Children in S.Africa," *Los Angeles Times*, December 18, 1992; see also, Ferial Hafferjee, "Children for whom a prison cell is home," *Weekly Mail and Guardian*, (Johannesburg) October 15 to 21, 1993. The number of juveniles held in detention fell towards the end of 1992, as a result of major campaign coordinated by several groups, including the Community Law Centre of the University of the Western Cape, Lawyers for Human Rights and NICRO-Cape Town, advocating children's and prisoners' rights. Lawyers for Human Rights ran a campaign to "Free a Child for Christmas" at the end of the year. However, LHR and NICRO reported that the number of children in prison increased again during 1993. A study of children in the criminal justice system, *Justice for the Children: No Child Should Be Caged*, was published by the Children's Rights Research and Advocacy Project of the Community Law Centre at the University of the Western Cape, on October 22, 1992.

[117] Child Care Act 1983, Section 28; Correctional Services Act 1959, Section 29.

[118] Since July 1992, Lawyers for Human Rights in Pietermaritzburg has run a Juvenile Justice Project, with one lawyer and one paralegal. Every child appearing in the Pietermaritzburg magistrate's court is contacted, and efforts are made to contact his or her parents. As a result children arrested in Pietermaritzburg rarely spend more than two or three nights in custody. There is no reason why a similar system could not be implemented by police at other police stations: interview with Ann Skelton, Regional Director of Lawyers for Human Rights, January 29, 1993.

31, 1991. Statistics are not kept noting the numbers of children held in police cells who are not ultimately charged.

Since the recent reforms took place, juveniles kept in prison or in police cells are usually, though not always, housed separately from adults. In some prisons we visited, for example in Kroonstad, this segregation had taken place only very recently, at the end of 1992. Moreover, despite residential segregation, children often mix with adults in exercise yards, as we saw in Modderbee and Kroonstad prisons; in addition, they may be transported to court with adult prisoners, as, for example, to and from Pollsmoor prison. In Pretoria Central prison, in Transkei and in some police lockups, we witnessed juvenile prisoners being housed with adults. All this raises serious security concerns. In addition, because anybody under twenty-one years of age is classified as a juvenile, sometimes very young and vulnerable children may be housed with individuals ten years older and potentially dangerous. In some cases, but not all, there is an effort to group children by age while holding them in custody. As is the case for adults, children awaiting trial are not segregated according to the type of offense with which they are charged, so that alleged murderers may be held in the same cells as shoplifters.

The mixing of children with adults, or with children of different age groups, is particularly serious in light of the disturbingly routine allegations of sexual abuse of juvenile prisoners.

Juvenile prisoners, like adults, are no longer officially segregated by race and should receive the same treatment whether white or black. However, the criminal justice system in general treats white children much more favorably than black, and very few white juveniles are sentenced to prison terms. The only white children we saw during our visits to South African prisons were white infants held with their mothers at women's prisons. Even more than white adults, white juveniles continue to receive preferential treatment.

In many prisons, the facilities for children are extremely poor, especially where there are only a few juveniles present. In Kroonstad, for example, no formal provision was made for the handful of children being held there to have any schooling. Some prisons, in particular Leeuwkop and Rustenberg, which we did not visit, reportedly have much more elaborate programs for children, including schooling and sports facilities. In a parallel situation to the women prisoners separated from their children, juveniles in custody, especially when they are held in these centralized facilities, may be held many miles from their places of residence, and effectively cut off from their families.

Children are among the victims of violence in police cells or prisons. Children are subject to the same disciplinary measures as adults, both authorized and unauthorized. In Modderbee prison in particular, juvenile prisoners stated to us that they were frequently assaulted and that they feared to talk to our representatives, even out of earshot of the warders, in case of reprisals. In a particularly shocking example, in October 1992, thirteen-year-old Neville Snyman was raped and killed by other juvenile offenders while being held awaiting trial in Robertson prison near Cape Town. He had spent two weeks in detention before appearing in court, when he was not released because his parents had not been able to attend court on the day of the hearing.[119]

The Department of Correctional Services has indicated that it does not wish to see children in prison. Yet the lack of an integrated approach to the criminal justice system means that prisons themselves have no control over the number of children sent to them. Measures proposed by the prison service to address concerns about juvenile offenders therefore focus on improved facilities rather than keeping children out of the system from the beginning.

SECURITY PRISONERS

Detention for interrogation or for preventive purposes is authorized under the Internal Security Act of 1982 and under equivalent legislation in the nominally independent homelands.[120] In addition, under the Public Safety Act of 1953, the state president may declare an emergency and promulgate emergency regulations allowing detention in other circumstances. During the emergency that was in force between 1985 and 1990, tens of thousands of South Africans were detained

---

[119] Community Law Centre, *Justice for the Children*, p.3.

[120] Section 29 of the Internal Security Act, the most notorious provision of the law, allowing detention for interrogation, was abolished in November 1993, by the Multiparty Negotiating Forum, and this change was ratified by the white parliament. However, other forms of detention under the ISA remain in effect.

without trial.[121] Mass long-term detention of this type has ceased, although emergency-type laws still apply in "unrest areas" declared by the government in many black townships.[122]

Extensive amendments to the Internal Security Act adopted in 1991 significantly improved the legal situation of security detainees, historically subject to extreme levels of abuse, and in most respects they became theoretically subject to the same treatment as unconvicted prisoners. In particular, the right of access to legal advice was restored. Detainees under the Internal Security Act or Unrest Regulations are generally held in police cells rather than prisons; they are therefore exposed to the same dangers of police brutality as others in police cells.

Until 1990, the Internal Security Act criminalized much extraparliamentary opposition activity, as well as membership of organizations such as the ANC or the South African Communist Party. Nelson Mandela was only the most famous of many black leaders held under this legislation. Security prisoners such as Mandela were generally segregated from other, purely criminal, offenders in high-security institutions such as Robben Island. Representatives of the International Committee of the Red Cross were permitted to visit security prisoners from 1964, but ceased doing so in 1989, when South Africa refused to give access to detainees held under emergency legislation.

After February 1990, when the ANC and other groups were unbanned and negotiations for a transition to majority rule began, it was agreed between the government and the ANC, in two "minutes" signed during 1990 at Groote Schuur and Pretoria, that prisoners held under this legislation should be released (see also the introduction to this report). By late 1993, approximately 1,600 prisoners had been released under these procedures. The Human Rights Commission stated at the

---

[121]An estimated 41,700 were detained under the emergency legislation between July 1985 and June 1990, with an additional 12,700 detained under the Internal Security Act over the same period: Human Rights Commission, Human Rights Update, June 1990.

[122]According to the Human Rights Commission, 1,093 people were detained under the unrest regulations or the Internal Security Act in 1991; 451 in 1992; and 609 in the first ten months of 1993 (284 in unrest areas, and the remainder under the ISA or equivalent legislation in the homelands); HRC, Human Rights Review 1992 and Monthly Repression Report, August 1993.

end of October 1993 that it believed that forty-six prisoners were still in custody who conformed to the description of political prisoner under the minutes. These prisoners are not segregated from other prisoners in any way, and are subject to the same conditions as prisoners convicted of criminal offenses with no political content.

JUDGMENT DEBTORS

South Africa is unusual in providing for the incarceration of judgment debtors; that is, persons against whom there is an outstanding judgment in a civil proceeding.[123] According to prison legislation, judgment debtors are supposed to be segregated from other prisoners; however, if this is not possible because of the small number of prisoners of the same category, judgment debtors may be housed with other unsentenced prisoners.[124] This was the case in those prisons visited by Human Rights Watch. In other respects, the conditions of their detention are similar to those for awaiting trial prisoners.

---

[123]For example, the leading international human rights treaty, the International Covenant on Civil and Political Rights, ratified by 124 countries (but not South Africa), provides in its Article 11 that "No one shall be imprisoned merely on the ground of inability to fulfil a contractual obligation."

[124]Correctional Services Regulations, Regulation 135.

XII. RELEASE

Until the reforms to the prison legislation passed in June 1993, the Commissioner of Correctional Services was empowered to remit any part of a prisoner's sentence, taking into account a recommendation by a prison board, and within general limits set by the president, but subject to no other control. The 1993 amendments substituted for this arbitrary decision a system of parole, to be administered by parole boards, whose members may include persons not employed by the department. More formal rules for parole are laid down, and the prisoner is given greater procedural protection. A system of "credits" is to be introduced, which a parole board may take into account when considering release of a prisoner.

In addition, and as described in the chapter on "Recent Changes in Prison Legislation," prisoners who have served part of their sentence may now be released into correctional supervision. While in correctional supervision, a prisoner may be ordered to perform community service, placed under house arrest, ordered to pay compensation to a victim, or undergo a treatment program.[125] The Department of Correctional Services claims a success rate of nearly 90 percent in implementing this program, though prisoners' rights organizations expressed concern to us as to its implementation in practice.

One of the conditions of parole may be that the prisoner should have a job. We were told by some prison warders and ex-prisoners that this system allowed for abuse, where the prison service found employment for prisoners with farmers and other private sector employers, who might exploit them. If prisoners complained at mistreatment they would be deemed to have broken parole, and could be returned to prison. Ex-prisoners also complained that their rights during parole were never explained to them, and that wages paid for the work they did amounted to as little as R.2.50 (US 80¢) a day. Prison warders at Modderbee prison who spoke to us before our visit stated that farmers who used parolees as labor would give gifts to prison staff in return for their access to prisoners. The Department of Correctional Services stated

---

[125]H.J. Bruyn, "An overview of the treatment of offenders in prison and correctional supervision," in Lorraine Glanz (ed), *Managing Crime in the New South Africa*, (Pretoria: Human Sciences Research Council, 1992).

to us that any prison warders caught engaging in such practices would be disciplined.

In theory, each prison has a pre-release counselling service. However, in the prisons we visited, mainly white prisoners were benefiting from such programs. At Kroonstad, where many white prisoners are housed, there were nine fully-qualified social workers for the whole prison, but only one was black and the others did not speak any African languages. Four auxiliary social workers were black. This lack of attention to black prisoners was acknowledged to be a problem by the prison staff. At Modderbee, there were only two fully qualified social workers and nine auxiliaries. At Barberton, there was only one fully qualified social worker, described by prisoners as "useless," and two auxiliary social workers for the whole prison complex. In Kroonstad women's prison, black women complained that the social worker did not understand nor spend as much time on their problems as on those of the white women. Each prisoner is given R.20 ($6.50) on release. The Department of Correctional Services pays fares home on public transportation.

The amnesties for both security-related and ordinary prisoners since 1990 have caused an outcry from parts of South Africa because of the mistaken release of at least one potentially violent criminal. This response led the government to announce in May 1993 that it would review the release of security prisoners released over the previous three years and take steps to rearrest those released in error. The amendments to the prisons legislation in June introduced a new section providing for the arrest and detention for seventy-two hours of a prisoner believed to have been erroneously released. The reincarceration of the prisoner would then require the approval of a judge.[126]

The early releases were also controversial within the prisons. Although the release of security prisoners was subject to an agreed review procedure, the date of release of ordinary prisoners was a purely executive decision. In most of the prisons we visited, prisoners expressed uncertainty as to the procedures by which early release was granted, and resentment at the selection process. In one case, a prisoner complained that his co-defendant, who had been sentenced to the death penalty, had

---

[126] Correctional Services Amendment Act 1993, Section 13, introducing Section 32A to the principal act.

been granted release, while he, with a lesser sentence, was still incarcerated. Hunger strikes and protests by prisoners hoping to be included in the programs for early release, mainly on political grounds, reached crisis proportions during 1991, and were still continuing in 1993 at the time of our visits.

In addition, it seemed that magistrates were attempting to circumvent the policy of granting early release by handing down longer sentences. On several occasions we heard anecdotal evidence that magistrates, who handle most criminal cases, had specifically mentioned recent releases in giving a long sentence to a convicted criminal. There is a need to integrate the release procedure with sentencing policy, to provide for a more formalized system for deciding which prisoners are able to benefit from general amnesties, and to ensure that all prisoners have the system clearly explained to them.

XIII. PRISONS IN THE "INDEPENDENT" HOMELANDS

An estimated 7.5 million South Africans live in the so-called independent homelands: Transkei, Ciskei, Bophuthatswana and Venda.[127] Each of these "independent" states has its own prison system. We were able to visit prisons in Bophuthatswana (Rooigrond) and Transkei (Umtata Central and Wellington). Our requests to visit prisons in Ciskei were ignored (we did not ask to visit in Venda).

Bophuthatswana, with an estimated population of 2.4 million, held an average of 2,217 prisoners during 1991 (the last year for which statistics were available), with a ratio significantly lower than that in South Africa generally, of ninety-two prisoners per 100,000.[128] In Transkei, at the time of our February 1993 visit, there were 1,752 prisoners, according to the authorities. With an estimated population of 3.46 million, the ratio per 100,000 inhabitants stood at fifty.[129]

Prisons in these two homelands were similar to those in South Africa, and followed similar regimes, but tended to be in worse physical condition. At the time of our visits in Bophuthatswana, the system had just introduced beds for all its inmates, but not pillows and sheets. In Transkei, prisoners slept on mats. Overcrowding was a problem in both prison systems visited.

In Transkei, overcrowding was particularly serious and conditions especially bad in the section of the men's prison that held those awaiting trial. The over-crowding was exacerbated and made more onerous for the

---

[127] As part of the system of "grand apartheid," South Africa created ten homelands, or *bantustans*, which were to form the sole focus of black political activity. In theory, all blacks would become citizens of a homeland created for their own ethnic group, and work in white South Africa only as migrant labor. Of the ten homelands, four — Transkei, Bophuthatswana, Venda and Ciskei — eventually became nominally independent, but the other six remained merely "self-governing territories," though there was little difference in practice.

[128] Annual Report of the Commissioner of Prisons, Republic of Bophuthatswana, Mmabatho, Bophuthatswana 1991.

[129] Population figures from *Race Relations Survey 1991/92*, South African Institute on Race Relations, Johannesburg, 1992, p. 2.

prisoners by delays in the system: we received reports of pre-trial detention for periods as long as two and three years. Also in Transkei, we received repeated complaints about the food, including reports of rotten fish in the Central Prison.

The Bophuthatswana prison system has a "privilege" classification system similar to that of South Africa proper. Inmates are classified in groups 1 through 5, with 5 having the most lenient regime. Inmates enter at level 2 and can advance one notch after six months. Under this system, depending on classification, inmates can receive between twenty-four and sixty visits per year, with the highest classification group allowed to have contact visits. Unlike in South Africa proper, the regulations provided for limits on the number of letters written and received by each classification. Prisoners could write between twenty-four and seventy-two letters; and receive between twelve and sixty letters a year. Groups 1 and 2 were not allowed to receive any periodicals, the remaining groups could receive up to two dailies, two magazines and two Sunday papers. In Transkei, South Africa's "privilege" system appears not to operate very efficiently, though it exists in theory.

In the Umtata prisons, we received reports from prisoners of assaults carried out by prison staff, and of inadequate medical attention being given to prisoners who had been assaulted or who were sick for other reasons. A number of prisoners complained of asthma, which was aggravated by damp cells and dirty bedding.

APPENDIX I

The Department of Correctional Services' Comments to Draft Recommendations by Human Rights Watch and HRW's Response

o **juveniles should never be housed in adult institutions;**
The Department of Correctional Services (DCS): "We have separate prisons for juveniles, specially designed according to their specific needs. However, due to overcrowding and the fact that the Department realises the importance to incarcerate juveniles as near as possible to their families, they are also housed in special sections of adult prisons."
> HRW: While it is true that, according to our observations, juveniles slept in separate sections of adult institutions, it was reported to us that they were transported to court along with adults and mingled with adults within the prison when not actually locked in their cells.

o **in institutions for juveniles, housing in separate age groups should always be a rule to avoid situations in which 10-year-olds might be housed with 21-year-olds;**
The Government: "This is already the policy of the Department."
> HRW: While glad that this is the policy of the Department, we received reliable reports that this is not always the practice and are concerned that opportunities for abuse of younger children remain.

o **all cases of alleged beatings of prisoners by guards or of collaboration by guards in the gang system should be thoroughly investigated and staff members found guilty of applying unauthorized force should be disciplined;**
The Government: "Every complaint of an assault, no matter how petty, is regarded in a serious light. Prisoners are daily given the opportunity to lodge any complaints. A Departmental enquiry into any alleged assault is instituted and suitable actions are taken. Serious assaults are reported to the South African Police for investigation in order that the legal process may take its normal course."
> HRW: We are aware of the existing mechanism for lodging complaints. According to repeated testimonies, however, in practice the mechanism often does not work. Many prisoners alleged that their complaints are not

taken seriously. We welcome the comment as a statement of intent.

o **there should be a thorough, independent investigation of the 1991 riot in Barberton prison, the six deaths and the subsequent alleged assaults against prisoners;**

The Government: "The legal process arising out of the incident at Barberton prison has already been activated and the results up to this stage can be analised and followed up by any individual, observer or any other interested party."

HRW: We know that a trial of fifteen prisoners charged with murder is coming up in February. As of this writing, we are not aware of a formal investigation of the alleged abuses against prisoners by prison staff members.

o **restraints should never be applied as a disciplinary measure; when used to subdue a prisoner, they should only be applied as long as strictly necessary, and never for more than a few hours;**

The Government: "We agree - this is already common practice in the prison services."

HRW: during our visits we observed at least one prisoner in disciplinary segregation with physical restraints as an additional punishment. We also received reports that they were in use as late as November 1993.

o **cell space should be used evenly within each prison to avoid creating artificial overcrowding;**

The Government: "We reject the submission that there is artificial overcrowding in SA prisons. The separation of prisoners with regard to sex, age, sentenced and unsentenced, legal grounds, personal safety of inmates dictates and necessitates that certain sections may be higher populated than others although a balance is being pursued at all times."

HRW: We acknowledge that some unevenness in the use of cell space is unavoidable for the reasons explained in the Government's response. But discrepancies in filling the space, as observed during visits to several prisons, were larger than needs suggested by the above reasons. We saw entirely empty cells in institutions where cells next door were vastly overcrowded, or just a few prisoners in a cell the same size as others holding up to forty people. We believe that the existing prison space could be used in a more efficient fashion.

o   **all cells should be equipped with basic furniture such as beds, chairs, tables and cabinets or shelves for private belongings;**

The DCS: "We agree - budgetary constraints dictate that this situation cannot be obtained overnight but we have a planned schedule at hand to work towards the goal."

       HRW: We welcome the Government's intent to provide
       basic furniture for prisoners.

o   **inmates should always be provided with three meals a day. Meal times should be spaced evenly during the day, to avoid excessively long periods between the last and the first meal of the day;**

The DCS: "All prisoners are provided with 3 meals a day. The importance to avoid excessively long periods between the last and first meal of the day is realised, but due to a shortage of staff members this is not possible. To alleviate this problem prisoners are given their light meal to the cells in the evening so that is can be eaten later. In your report reference is made of this practice."

       HRW: Shortage of staff does not justify the current
       practice. Efforts should be made to increase the number
       of staff members and to eliminate the long periods
       between the last and the first meals of the day.

o   **all prisoners should have at a minimum, an hour of daily exercise;**

The DCS: "This is the policy and also stated in our orders. Where this does not happen in practice it is due to overcrowding and a shortage of staff members."

       HRW: As above, efforts should be made to correct this
       situation either through changes in the management or
       by employing more staff. Shortage of staff does not
       justify violations of basic prison standards.

o   **the provision making it an infraction to discuss prison conditions during visits should be removed from prison regulations;**

The DCS: "There is no provision in the prison regulations forbidding prisoners to discuss prison conditions during visits."

       HRW: During our 1993 visit to one of the prisons we
       saw and photographed a sign in a visiting room
       specifically prohibiting any discussions of prison
       conditions (we refer to this fact in the report).

o   **paralegals and trainee attorneys should be allowed equal access to prisoners as fully qualified attorneys or advocates;**
The DCS: "This is common practice."
> HRW: Although some organizations have made individual arrangements with the Department for paralegals to have access to prisoners, access is not granted as a right, as is the case with qualified attorneys.

o   **efforts should be made to house prisoners as near to their area of residence as possible, and all requests for transfers should be sympathetically assessed;**
The DCS: "Although the importance of family ties is realised overcrowding prohibits the Department of achieving this goal in all circumstances. However, in the planning of new prisons and the construction thereof cognisance is taken of these realities. The Department considers all representations by inmates in a sympathetic manner."
> HRW: One of the most frequent complaints voiced to us by prisoners was that their requests for transfers were either ignored or resulted in reprisals.

o   **for prisoners whose relatives must travel in order to visit, it should be possible to combine several shorter visits into a longer one or to conduct several visits in just a few days when visiting relatives are staying in the area where the prison is located;**
The DCS: "This is being practised by heads of prisons and form part of the operational order of the Department."
> HRW: Rather than leaving it to the discretion of individual heads of prisons, this should be a policy of the entire South African prison system.

o   **prisoners of all races and both sexes should have equal access to vocational training and to the most desirable prison jobs;**
The DCS: "The accessibility to training and jobs are based on security classification, ability and qualification and not on the grounds of race or sex taking into account that males and females are separated in the prison environment. As is the policy in most prisons all over the world prisoners of different sexes are separated and therefor it is not possible to give prisoners of both sexes access to the same training and prison jobs. Work normally done by women and men differ [sic] and therefor the same training facilities are not made available to them."

> HRW: We are not quite sure what the Government means by stating that "work normally done by men and women differ." As we state in the report, we noticed that the vocational training to acquire well paid professions was available to men only, while women did the laundry, washing, and sewing, as well as some beauty salon training.

o   **vocational training of a meaningful nature should be progressively expanded, ideally to be available to all prisoners;**

The DCS: "A new vocational training system was designed during 1991/92 in conjunction with various Training Boards. It is based on modular skills training and according to circumstances a prisoner completes the number of modules possible. This enables the Department to develop the labour capacity of all prisoners with long and short term sentences by means of affordable, career-orientated and market-related training programmes. This however remains an expensive way of training and all prisoners do not qualify on grounds of aptitude and qualifications.

"Furthermore there are formal skills training for those prisoners who have already reached the minimum period of their detention to be trained by Training Centres and by instructors of the Department under the scheme for unemployed persons."

> HRW: We welcome the existence of the plan. During our visits in 1992 and 1993 we did not hear a single reference to this plan from prisoners, which suggests that it was not being widely implemented and known at the time. Most prisoners were not receiving training of any kind. As stated earlier, we believe that any investment in prisoners' education is money well spent that will eventually pay off to the society.

o   **prisoners should be encouraged to study not only on the most basic level. Efforts should be made to facilitate access to correspondence courses for all prisoners who are willing to study;**

The DCS: "It is the policy of the Department and forms part of the functions of the qualified educational staff members to encourage prisoners to participate in educational programmes. They are furthermore encouraged by the Institutional committee. All prisoners do have access to correspondence course with the only prerequisite being that they must have the financial abilities to pay for their tuition. (Please also see the comment with regard to the education of prisoners.)"

> HRW: By "facilitating access" we mean making it financially possible as well, in addition to simply authorizing enrollment in correspondence courses. Many prisoners expressed sadness to us at their own inability to pay for education. As stated above, we believe the money spent in this way would be a sound investment for South Africa.

o **training for prison warders should place emphasis on conflict resolution and respect for prisoners' rights rather than the simple enforcement of discipline;**

The DCS: "The matter of dealing with conflict as well as the methods of resolving conflict is embodied in the curricula of all Departmental training and development courses. The enforcement of discipline is but only one element in the basic training course of members."

> HRW: Prison staff members in various institutions expressed their concerns to us that their training overemphasized the use of force and lacked instruction regarding conflict resolution.

o **an effort should be made to integrate reforms in the prison system with reforms in the general criminal justice system, so that, for example, efforts to reduce the prison population do not result in longer sentences being imposed by magistrates;**

The DCS: "The criminal justice system in South Africa is a well coordinated entity and there is no indication that longer prison terms are being imposed by courts to jeopardize efforts to reduce the growthrate of the prison population. Alternative sentencing options such as correctional supervision is extensively used by the courts. This has resulted in a slower growth rate in the prison population than otherwise would be the case if this system was not in place, or if the courts did not endorse or use this system adequately.

An interdepartmental Crime Prevention Secretariate was established between the Department of Correctional Services, Police and Justice to further the close cooperation within the Criminal Justice System."

> HRW: The alternative sentencing, while a welcome approach, is still in an early stage of its application, and its impact on the overall rate of imprisonment in the

country is not significant. The assertion that the prison population grew more slowly than it would have without the new sentencing options is not supported by evidence; in the past two years — that is, precisely when new sentencing options were being introduced — the country's prison population grew significantly.

o   **all cases of abuse of the parole system by prison staff should be fully investigated and those involved disciplined. The criteria for early release or parole should be clearly explained to prisoners, and uniformly applied across the system.**

The DCS: "Agreed. Any member who oversteps his authority or abuses a parolee or inmate is disciplined. Any specific evidence will be used in this regard.

The release of a prisoner on parole is not determined by a single member and each release is dealt with by the Institutional Committee and the Parole Board. Various safeguards to protect the right of the prisoner and community are built into the system.

The placement of inmates on parole is a long standing practice and is well known to inmates as well as the various institutional committees/release boards dealing with this matter. Furthermore release policy is the product of advice rendered by the Advisory Council on Correctional Services chaired by a judge of the Supreme Court of South Africa and where no governmental bodies have an input. Information on release policy is distributed as widely as possible under prisoners, bearing in mind that new prisoners are admitted to the system all the time. In this process it is inevitable that at any given time some inmates are better informed than others. The Department however also makes use of all methods at its disposal to inform relevant parties in this regard."

HRW: We received reports of abuses of the parole system. We welcome the news that the Government is working to improve the parole system.

APPENDIX II

STANDARD MINIMUM RULES
FOR THE TREATMENT OF PRISONERS

Adopted by the First United Nations Congress on the Prevention of Crime and the Treatment of Offenders, held at Geneva in 1955, and approved by the Economic and Social Council by its resolutions 663 C (XXIV) of 31 July 1957 and 2076 (LXII) of 13 May 1977

PRELIMINARY OBSERVATIONS

1. The following rules are not intended to describe in detail a model system of penal institutions. They seek only, on the basis of the general consensus of contemporary thought and the essential elements of the most adequate systems of today, to set out what is generally accepted as being good principle and practice in the treatment of prisoners and the management of institutions.

2. In view of the great variety of legal, social, economic and geographical conditions of the world, it is evident that not all of the rules are capable of application in all places and at all times. They should, however, serve to stimulate a constant endeavour to overcome practical difficulties in the way of their application, in the knowledge that they represent, as a whole, the minimum conditions which are accepted as suitable by the United Nations.

3. On the other hand, the rules cover a field in which thought is constantly developing. They are not intended to preclude experiment and practices, provided these are in harmony with the principles and seek to further the purposes which derive from the text of the rules as a whole. It will always be justifiable for the central prison administration to authorize departures from the rules in this spirit.

4. (1) Part I of the rules covers the general management of institutions, and is applicable to all categories of prisoners, criminal or civil, untried or convicted, including prisoners subject to "security measures or corrective measures ordered by the judge.

(2) Part 11 contains rules applicable only to the special categories dealt with in each section. Nevertheless, the rules under section A, applicable to prisoners under sentence, shall be equally applicable to categories of prisoners dealt with in sections B, C and D, provided they do not conflict with the rules governing those categories and are for their benefit.

5. (1) The rules do not seek to regulate the management of institutions set aside for young persons such as Borstal institutions or correctional schools, but in general part I would be equally applicable in such institutions.

(2) The category of young prisoners should include at least all young persons who come within the jurisdiction of juvenile courts. As a rule, such young persons should not be sentenced to imprisonment.

PART I

RULES OF GENERAL APPLICATION

Basic principle

6. (1) The following rules shall be applied impartially. There shall be no discrimination on grounds of race, colour, sex, language, religion, political or other opinion, national or social origin, property, birth or other status.

(2) On the other hand, it is necessary to respect the religious beliefs and moral precepts of the group to which a prisoner belongs.

Register

7. (1) In every place where persons are imprisoned there shall be kept a bound registration book with numbered pages in which shall be entered in respect of each prisoner received:

(a) Information concerning his identity;

(b) The reasons for his commitment and the authority therefor;

(c) The day and hour of his admission and release.

(2) No person shall be received in an institution without a valid commitment order of which the details shall have been previously entered in the register.

Separation of categories

8. The different categories of prisoners shall be kept in separate institutions or parts of institutions taking account of their sex, age, criminal record, the legal reason for their detention and the necessities of their treatment. Thus,

(a) Men and women shall so far as possible be detained in separate institutions; in an institution which receives both men and women the whole of the premises allocated to women shall be entirely separate;

(b) Untried prisoners shall be kept separate from convicted prisoners;

(c) Persons imprisoned for debt and other civil prisoners shall be kept separate from persons imprisoned by reason of a criminal offence;

(d) Young prisoners shall be kept separate from adults.

Accommodation

9. (1) Where sleeping accommodation is in individual cells or rooms, each prisoner shall occupy by night a cell or room by himself.

If for special reasons, such as temporary overcrowding, it becomes necessary for the central prison administration to make an exception to this rule, it is not desirable to have two prisoners in a cell or room.

(2) Where dormitories are used, they shall be occupied by prisoners carefully selected as being suitable to associate with one another in those conditions. There shall be regular supervision by night, in keeping with the nature of the institution.

10. All accommodation provided for the use of prisoners and in particular all sleeping accommodation shall meet all requirements of health, due regard being paid to climatic conditions and particularly to cubic content of air, minimum floor space, lighting, heating and ventilation.

11. In all places where prisoners are required to live or work,
(a) The windows shall be large enough to enable the prisoners to read or work by natural light, and shall be so constructed that they can allow the entrance of fresh air whether or not there is artificial ventilation;
(b) Artificial light shall be provided sufficient for the prisoners to read or work without injury to eyesight.

12. The sanitary installations shall be adequate to enable every prisoner to comply with the needs of nature when necessary and in a clean and decent manner.

13. Adequate bathing and shower installations shall be provided so that every prisoner may be enabled and required to have a bath or shower, at a temperature suitable to the climate, as frequently as necessary for general hygiene according to season and geographical region, but at least once a week in a temperate climate.

14. All parts of an institution regularly used by prisoners shall be properly maintained and kept scrupulously clean at all times.

Personal hygiene

15. Prisoners shall be required to keep their persons clean, and to this end they shall be provided with water and with such toilet articles as are necessary for health and cleanliness.

16. In order that prisoners may maintain a good appearance compatible with their self-respect, facilities shall be provided for the proper care of the hair and beard, and men shall be enabled to shave regularly.

Clothing and bedding

17. (1) Every prisoner who is not allowed to wear his own clothing shall be provided with an outfit of clothing suitable for the climate and adequate to keep him in good health. Such clothing shall in no manner be degrading or humiliating.

(2) All clothing shall be clean and kept in proper condition. Underclothing shall be changed and washed as often as necessary for the maintenance of hygiene.

(3) In exceptional circumstances, whenever a prisoner is removed outside the institution for an authorized purpose, he shall be allowed to wear his own clothing or other inconspicuous clothing.

18. If prisoners are allowed to wear their own clothing, arrangements shall be made on their admission to the institution to ensure that it shall be clean and fit for use.

19. Every prisoner shall, in accordance with local or national standards, be provided with a separate bed, and with separate and sufficient bedding which shall be clean when issued, kept in good order and changed often enough to ensure its cleanliness.

Food

20. (1) Every prisoner shall be provided by the administration at the usual hours with food of nutritional value adequate for health and strength, of wholesome quality and well prepared and served.

(2) Drinking water shall be available to every prisoner whenever he needs it.

Exercise and sport

21. (1) Every prisoner who is not employed in outdoor work shall have at least one hour of suitable exercise in the open air daily if the weather permits.

(2) Young prisoners, and others of suitable age and physique, shall receive physical and recreational training during the period of exercise. To this end space, installations and equipment should be provided.

Medical services

22. (1) At every institution there shall be available the services of at least one qualified medical officer who should have some knowledge of psychiatry. The medical services should be organized in close relationship to the general health administration of the community or nation. They shall include a psychiatric service for the diagnosis and, in proper cases, the treatment of states of mental abnormality.

(2) Sick prisoners who require specialist treatment shall be transferred to specialized institutions or to civil hospitals. Where hospital facilities are provided in an institution, their equipment, furnishings and pharmaceutical supplies shall be proper for the medical care and treatment of sick prisoners, and there shall be a staff of suitable trained officers.

(3) The services of a qualified dental officer shall be available to every prisoner.

23. (1) In women's institutions there shall be special accommodation for all necessary pre-natal and post-natal care and treatment. Arrangements shall be made wherever practicable for children to be born in a hospital outside the institution. If a child is born in prison, this fact shall not be mentioned in the birth certificate.

(2) Where nursing infants are allowed to remain in the institution with their mothers, provision shall be made for a nursery staffed by qualified persons, where the infants shall be placed when they are not in the care of their mothers.

24. The medical officer shall see and examine every prisoner as soon as possible after his admission and thereafter as necessary, with a view particularly to the discovery of physical or mental illness and the taking of all necessary measures; the segregation of prisoners suspected of infectious or contagious conditions; the noting of physical or mental defects which might hamper rehabilitation, and the determination of the physical capacity of every prisoner for work.

25. (1) The medical officer shall have the care of the physical and mental health of the prisoners and should daily see all sick prisoners, all who complain of illness, and any prisoner to whom his attention is specially directed.

(2) The medical officer shall report to the director whenever he considers that a prisoner's physical or mental health has been or will be injuriously affected by continued imprisonment or by any condition of imprisonment.

26. (1) The medical officer shall regularly inspect and advise the director upon:

    (a) The quantity, quality, preparation and service of food;

    (b) The hygiene and cleanliness of the institution and the prisoners;

(c) The sanitation, heating, lighting and ventilation of the institution;

(d) The suitability and cleanliness of the prisoners' clothing and bedding;

(e) The observance of the rules concerning physical education and sports, in cases where there is no technical personnel in charge of these activities.

(2) The director shall take into consideration the reports and advice that the medical officer submits according to rules 25 (2) and 26 and, in case he concurs with the recommendations made, shall take immediate steps to give effect to those recommendations; if they are not within his competence or if he does not concur with them, he shall immediately submit his own report and the advice of the medical officer to higher authority.

Discipline and punishment

27. Discipline and order shall be maintained with firmness, but with no more restriction than is necessary for safe custody and well-ordered community life.

28. (1) No prisoner shall be employed, in the service of the institution, in any disciplinary capacity.

(2) This rule shall not, however, impede the proper functioning of systems based on self-government, under which specified social, educational or sports activities or responsibilities are entrusted, under supervision, to prisoners who are formed into groups for the purposes of treatment.

29. The following shall always be determined by the law or by the regulation of the competent administrative authority:
(a) Conduct constituting a disciplinary offence;
(b) The types and duration of punishment which may be inflicted;
(c) The authority competent to impose such punishment.

30. (1) No prisoner shall be punished except in accordance with the terms of such law or regulation, and never twice for the same offence.

(2) No prisoner shall be punished unless he has been informed of the offence alleged against him and given a proper opportunity of presenting his defence. The competent authority shall conduct a thorough examination of the case.

(3) Where necessary and practicable the prisoner shall be allowed to make his defence through an interpreter.

31. Corporal punishment, punishment by placing in a dark cell, and all cruel, inhuman or degrading punishments shall be completely prohibited as punishments for disciplinary offences.

32. (1) Punishment by close confinement or reduction of diet shall never be inflicted unless the medical officer has examined the prisoner and certified in writing that he is fit to sustain it.

(2) The same shall apply to any other punishment that may be prejudicial to the physical or mental health of a prisoner. In no case may such punishment be contrary to or depart from the principle stated in rule 31.

(3) The medical officer shall visit daily prisoners undergoing such punishments and shall advise the director if he considers the termination or alteration of the punishment necessary on grounds of physical or mental health.

Instruments of restraint

33. Instruments of restraint, such as handcuffs, chains, irons and straitjackets, shall never be applied as a punishment. Furthermore, chains or irons shall not be used as restraints. Other instruments of restraint shall not be used except in the following circumstances:

(a) As a precaution against escape during a transfer, provided that they shall be removed when the prisoner appears before a judicial or administrative authority;

(b) On medical grounds by direction of the medical officer;

(c) By order of the director, if other methods of control fail, in order to prevent a prisoner from injuring himself or others or from damaging property; in such instances the director shall at once consult the medical officer and report to the higher administrative authority.

34. The patterns and manner of use of instruments of restraint shall be decided by the central prison administration. Such instruments must not be applied for any longer time than is strictly necessary.

Information to and complaints by prisoners

35. (1) Every prisoner on admission shall be provided with written information about the regulations governing the treatment of prisoners of his category, the disciplinary requirements of the institution, the authorized methods of seeking information and making complaints, and all such other matters as are necessary to enable him to understand both his rights and his obligations and to adapt himself to the life of the institution.

(2) If a prisoner is illiterate, the aforesaid information shall be conveyed to him orally.

36. (1) Every prisoner shall have the opportunity each week day of making requests or complaints to the director of the institution or the officer authorized to represent him.

(2) It shall be possible to make requests or complaints to the inspector of prisons during his inspection. The prisoner shall have the opportunity to talk to the inspector or to any other inspecting officer without the director or other members of the staff being present.

(3) Every prisoner shall be allowed to make a request or complaint, without censorship as to substance but in proper form, to the central prison administration, the judicial authority or other proper authorities through approved channels.

(4) Unless it is evidently frivolous or groundless, every request or complaint shall be promptly dealt with and replied to without undue delay.

Contact with the outside world

37. Prisoners shall be allowed under necessary supervision to communicate with their family and reputable friends at regular intervals, both by correspondence and by receiving visits.

38. (1) Prisoners who are foreign nationals shall be allowed reasonable facilities to communicate with the diplomatic and consular representatives of the State to which they belong.

(2) Prisoners who are nationals of States without diplomatic or consular representation in the country and refugees or stateless persons shall be allowed similar facilities to communicate with the diplomatic representative of the State which takes charge of their interests or any national or international authority whose task it is to protect such persons.

39. Prisoners shall be kept informed regularly of the more important items of news by the reading of newspapers, periodicals or special institutional publications, by hearing wireless transmissions, by lectures or by any similar means as authorized or controlled by the administration.

Books

40. Every institution shall have a library for the use of all categories of prisoners, adequately stocked with both recreational and instructional books, and prisoners shall he encouraged to make full use of it.

Religion

41. (1) If the institution contains a sufficient number of prisoners of the same religion, a qualified representative of that religion shall be appointed or approved. If the number of prisoners justifies it and conditions permit, the arrangement should be on a full-time basis.

(2) A qualified representative appointed or approved under paragraph (1) shall be allowed to hold regular services and to pay pastoral visits in private to prisoners of his religion at proper times.

(3) Access to a qualified representative of any religion shall not be refused to any prisoner. On the other hand, if any prisoner should object to a visit of any religious representative, his attitude shall be fully respected.

42. So far as practicable, every prisoner shall be allowed to satisfy the needs of his religious life by attending the services provided in the institution and having in his possession the books of religious observance and instruction of his denomination.

Retention of prisoners' property

43. (1) All money, valuables, clothing and other effects belonging to a prisoner which under the regulations of the institution he is not allowed to retain shall on his admission to the institution be placed in safe custody. An inventory thereof shall be signed by the prisoner. Steps shall be taken to keep them in good condition.

(2) On the release of the prisoner all such articles and money shall be returned to him except in so far as he has been authorized to spend money or send any such property out of the institution, or it has been found necessary on hygienic grounds to destroy any article of clothing. The prisoner shall sign a receipt for the articles and money returned to him.

(3) Any money or effects received for a prisoner from outside shall be treated in the same way.

(4) If a prisoner brings in any drugs or medicine, the medical officer shall decide what use shall be made of them.

Notification of death, illness, transfer, etc.

44. (1) Upon the death or serious illness of, or serious injury to a prisoner, or his removal to an institution for the treatment of mental affections, the director shall at once inform the spouse, if the prisoner is married, or the nearest relative and shall in any event inform any other person previously designated by the prisoner.

(2) A prisoner shall be informed at once of the death or serious illness of any near relative. In case of the critical illness of a near relative, the prisoner should be authorized, whenever circumstances allow, to go to his bedside either under escort or alone.

(3) Every prisoner shall have the right to inform at once his family of his imprisonment or his transfer to another institution.

Removal of prisoners

45. (1) When the prisoners are being removed to or from an institution they shall be exposed to public view as little as possible, and proper safeguards shall be adopted to protect them from insult, curiosity and publicity in any form.

(2) The transport of prisoners in conveyances with inadequate ventilation or light, or in any way which would subject them to unnecessary physical hardship, shall be prohibited.

(3) The transport of prisoners shall be carried out at the expense of the administration and equal conditions shall obtain for all of them.

Institutional personnel

46. (1) The prison administration, shall provide for the careful selection of every grade of the personnel, since it is on their integrity, humanity, professional capacity and personal suitability for the work that the proper administration of the institutions depends.

(2) The prison administration shall constantly seek to awaken and maintain in the minds both of the personnel and of the public the conviction that this work is a social service of great importance, and to this end all appropriate means of informing the public should be used.

(3) To secure the foregoing ends, personnel shall be appointed on a full-time basis as professional prison officers and have civil service status with security of tenure subject only to good conduct, efficiency and physical fitness. Salaries shall be adequate to attract and retain suitable men and women; employment benefits and conditions of service shall be favourable in view of the exacting nature of the work.

47. (1) The personnel shall possess an adequate standard of education and intelligence.

(2) Before entering on duty, the personnel shall be given a course of training in their general and specific duties and be required to pass theoretical and practical tests.

(3) After entering on duty and during their career, the personnel shall maintain and improve their knowledge and professional capacity by attending courses of in-service training to be organized at suitable intervals.

48. All members of the personnel shall at all times so conduct themselves and perform their duties as to influence the prisoners for good by their example and to command their respect.

49. (1) So far as possible, the personnel shall include a sufficient number of specialists such as psychiatrists, psychologists, social workers, teachers and trade instructors.

(2) The services of social workers, teachers and trade instructors shall be secured on a permanent basis, without thereby excluding part-time or voluntary workers.

50. (1) The director of an institution should be adequately qualified for his task by character, administrative ability, suitable training and experience.

(2) He shall devote his entire time to his official duties and shall not be appointed on a part-time basis.

(3) He shall reside on the premises of the institution or in its immediate vicinity.

(4) When two or more institutions are under the authority of one director, he shall visit each of them at frequent intervals. A responsible resident official shall be in charge of each of these institutions.

51. (1) The director, his deputy, and the majority of the other personnel of the institution shall be able to speak the language of the greatest number of prisoners, or a language understood by the greatest number of them.

(2) Whenever necessary, the services of an interpreter shall be used.

52. (1) In institutions which are large enough to require the services of one or more full-time medical officers, at least one of them shall reside on the premises of the institution or in its immediate vicinity.

(2) In other institutions the medical officer shall visit daily and shall reside near enough to be able to attend without delay in cases of urgency.

53. (1) In an institution for both men and women, the part of the institution set aside for women shall be under the authority of a responsible woman officer who shall have the custody of the keys of all that part of the institution.

(2) No male member of the staff shall enter the part of the institution set aside for women unless accompanied by a woman officer.

(3) Women prisoners shall be attended and supervised only by women officers. This does not, however, preclude male members of the staff, particularly doctors and teachers, from carrying out their professional duties in institutions or parts of institutions set aside for women.

54. (1) Officers of the institutions shall not, in their relations with the prisoners, use force except in self-defence or in cases of attempted escape, or active or passive physical resistance to an order based on law or regulations. Officers who have recourse to force must use no more than is strictly necessary and must report the incident immediately to the director of the institution.

(2) Prison officers shall be given special physical training to enable them to restrain aggressive prisoners.

(3) Except in special circumstances, staff performing duties which bring them into direct contact with prisoners should not be armed. Furthermore, staff should in no circumstances be provided with arms unless they have been trained in their use.

Inspection

55. There shall be a regular inspection of penal institutions and services by qualified and experienced inspectors appointed by a competent authority. Their task shall be in particular to ensure that these institutions are administered in accordance with existing laws and regulations and with a view to bringing about the objectives of penal and correctional services.

PART II

RULES APPLICABLE TO SPECIAL CATEGORIES

A. PRISONERS UNDER SENTENCE

Guiding principles

56. The guiding principles hereafter are intended to show the spirit in which penal institutions should be administered and the purposes at which they should aim, in accordance with the declaration made under Preliminary Observation I of the present text.

57. Imprisonment and other measures which result in cutting off an offender from the outside world are afflictive by the very fact of taking from the person the right of self-determination by depriving him of his liberty. Therefore the prison system shall not, except as incidental to justifiable segregation or the maintenance of discipline, aggravate the suffering inherent in such a situation.

58. The purpose and justification of a sentence of imprisonment or a similar measure deprivative of liberty is ultimately to protect society against crime. This end can only be achieved if the period of imprisonment is used to ensure, so far as possible, that upon his return to society the offender is not only willing but able to lead a law-abiding and self-supporting life.

59. To this end, the institution should utilize all the remedial, educational, moral, spiritual and other forces and forms of assistance which are appropriate and available, and should seek to apply them according to the individual treatment needs of the prisoners.

60. (1) The regime of the institution should seek to minimize any differences between prison life and life at liberty which tend to lessen the responsibility of the prisoners or the respect due to their dignity as human beings.

(2) Before the completion of the sentence, it is desirable that the necessary steps be taken to ensure for the prisoner a gradual return to life in society. This aim may be achieved, depending on the case, by a pre-release regime organized in the same institution or in another appropriate institution, or by release on trial under some kind of supervision which must not be entrusted to the police but should be combined with effective social aid.

61. The treatment of prisoners should emphasize not their exclusion from the community, but their continuing part in it. Community agencies should, therefore, be enlisted wherever possible to assist the staff of the institution in the task of social rehabilitation of the prisoners. There should be in connection with every institution social workers charged with the duty of maintaining and improving all desirable relations of a prisoner with his family and with valuable social agencies. Steps should be taken to safeguard, to the maximum extent compatible with the law and the sentence, the rights relating to civil interests, social security rights and other social benefits of prisoners.

62. The medical services of the institution shall seek to detect and shall treat any physical or mental illnesses or defects which may hamper a prisoner's rehabilitation. All necessary medical, surgical and psychiatric services shall be provided to that end.

63. (1) The fulfilment of these principles requires individualization of treatment and for this purpose a flexible system of classifying prisoners in groups; it is therefore desirable that such groups should be distributed in separate institutions suitable for the treatment of each group.

(2) These institutions need not provide the same degree of security for every group. It is desirable to provide varying degrees of security according to the needs of different groups. Open institutions, by the very fact that they provide no physical security against escape but rely on the self-discipline of the inmates, provide the conditions most favourable to rehabilitation for carefully selected prisoners.

(3) It is desirable that the number of prisoners in closed institutions should not be so large that the individualization of treatment

is hindered. In some countries it is considered that the population of such institutions should not exceed five hundred. In open institutions the population should be as small as possible.

(4) On the other hand, it is undesirable to maintain prisons which are so small that proper facilities cannot be provided.

64. The duty of society does not end with a prisoner's release. There should, therefore, be governmental or private agencies capable of lending the released prisoner efficient after-care directed towards the lessening of prejudice against him and towards his social rehabilitation.

Treatment

65. The treatment of persons sentenced to imprisonment or a similar measure shall have as its purpose, so far as the length of the sentence permits, to establish in them the will to lead law-abiding and self-supporting lives after their release and to fit them to do so. The treatment shall be such as will encourage their self-respect and develop their sense of responsibility.

66. (1) To these ends, all appropriate means shall be used, including religious care in the countries where this is possible, education, vocational guidance and training, social casework, employment counselling, physical development and strengthening of moral character, in accordance with the individual needs of each prisoner, taking account of his social and criminal history, his physical and mental capacities and aptitudes, his personal temperament, the length of his sentence and his prospects after release.

(2) For every prisoner with a sentence of suitable length, the director shall receive, as soon as possible after his admission, full reports on all the matters referred to in the foregoing paragraph. Such reports shall always include a report by a medical officer, wherever possible qualified in psychiatry, on the physical and mental condition of the prisoner.

(3) The reports and other relevant documents shall be placed in an individual file. This file shall be kept up to date and classified in such a way that it can be consulted by the responsible personnel whenever the need arises.

Classification and individualization

67. The purposes of classification shall be:

(a) To separate from others those prisoners who, by reason of their criminal records or bad characters, are likely to exercise a bad influence;

(b) To divide the prisoners into classes in order to facilitate their treatment with a view to their social rehabilitation.

68. So far as possible separate institutions or separate sections of an institution shall be used for the treatment of the different classes of prisoners.

69. As soon as possible after admission and after a study of the personality of each prisoner with a sentence of suitable length, a programme of treatment shall be prepared for him in the light of the knowledge obtained about his individual needs, his capacities and dispositions.

Privileges

70. Systems of privileges appropriate for the different classes of prisoners and the different methods of treatment shall be established at every institution, in order to encourage good conduct, develop a sense of responsibility and secure the interest and co-operation of the prisoners in their treatment.

Work

71. (1) Prison labour must not be of an afflictive nature.

(2) All prisoners under sentence shall be required to work, subject to their physical and mental fitness as determined by the medical officer.

(3) Sufficient work of a useful nature shall be provided to keep prisoners actively employed for a normal working day.

(4) So far as possible the work provided shall be such as will maintain or increase the prisoners' ability to earn an honest living after release.

(5) Vocational training in useful trades shall be provided for prisoners able to profit thereby and especially for young prisoners.

(6) Within the limits compatible with proper vocational selection and with the requirements of institutional administration and discipline, the prisoners shall be able to choose the type of work they wish to perform.

72.   (1) The organization and methods of work in the institutions shall resemble as closely as possible those of similar work outside institutions, so as to prepare prisoners for the conditions of normal occupational life.

(2) The interests of the prisoners and of their vocational training, however, must not be subordinated to the purpose of making a financial profit from an industry in the institution.

73.   (1) Preferably institutional industries and farms should be operated directly by the administration and not by private contractors.

(2) Where prisoners are employed in work not controlled by the administration, they shall always be under the supervision of the institution's personnel. Unless the work is for other departments of the government the full normal wages for such work shall be paid to the administration by the persons to whom the labour is supplied, account being taken of the output of the prisoners.

74. (1) The precautions laid down to protect the safety and health of free workmen shall be equally observed in institutions.

(2) Provision shall be made to indemnify prisoners against industrial injury, including occupational disease, on terms not less favourable than those extended by law to free workmen.

75. (1) The maximum daily and weekly working hours of the prisoners shall be fixed by law or by administrative regulation, taking into account local rules or custom in regard to the employment of free workmen.

(2) The hours so fixed shall leave one rest day a week and sufficient time for education and other activities required as part of the treatment and rehabilitation of the prisoners.

76. (1) There shall be a system of equitable remuneration of the work of prisoners.

(2) Under the system prisoners shall be allowed to spend at least a part of their earnings on approved articles for their own use and to send a part of their earnings to their family.

(3) The system should also provide that a part of the earnings should be set aside by the administration so as to constitute a savings fund to be handed over to the prisoner on his release.

Education and recreation

77. (1) Provision shall be made for the further education of all prisoners capable of profiting thereby, including religious instruction in the countries where this is possible. The education of illiterates and young prisoners shall be compulsory and special attention shall be paid to it by the administration.

(2) So far as practicable, the education of prisoners shall be integrated with the educational system of the country so that after their release they may continue their education without difficulty.

78. Recreational and cultural activities shall be provided in all institutions for the benefit of the mental and physical health of prisoners.

Social relations and after-care

79. Special attention shall be paid to the maintenance and improvement of such relations between a prisoner and his family as are desirable in the best interests of both.

80. From the beginning of a prisoner's sentence consideration shall be given to his future after release and he shall be encouraged and assisted to maintain or establish such relations with persons or agencies outside the institution as may promote the best interests of his family and his own social rehabilitation.

81. (1) Services and agencies, governmental or otherwise, which assist released prisoners to re-establish themselves in society shall ensure, so far as is possible and necessary, that released prisoners be provided with appropriate documents and identification papers, have suitable homes and work to go to, are suitably and adequately clothed having regard to the climate and season, and have sufficient means to reach their destination and maintain themselves in the period immediately following their release.

(2) The approved representatives of such agencies shall have all necessary access to the institution and to prisoners and shall be taken into consultation as to the future of a prisoner from the beginning of his sentence.

(3) It is desirable that the activities of such agencies shall be centralized or co-ordinated as far as possible in order to secure the best use of their efforts.

B. INSANE AND MENTALLY ABNORMAL PRISONERS

82. (1) Persons who are found to be insane shall not be detained in prisons and arrangements shall be made to remove them to mental institutions as soon as possible.

(2) Prisoners who suffer from other mental diseases or abnormalities shall be observed and treated in specialized institutions under medical management.

(3) During their stay in a prison, such prisoners shall be placed under the special supervision of a medical officer.

(4) The medical or psychiatric service of the penal institutions shall provide for the psychiatric treatment of all other prisoners who are in need of such treatment.

83. It is desirable that steps should be taken, by arrangement with the appropriate agencies, to ensure if necessary the continuation of psychiatric treatment after release and the provision of social-psychiatric after-care.

C. PRISONERS UNDER ARREST OR AWAITING TRIAL

84. (1) Persons arrested or imprisoned by reason of a criminal charge against them, who are detained either in police custody or in prison custody (jail) but have not yet been tried and sentenced, will be referred to as "untried prisoners" hereinafter in these rules.

(2) Unconvicted prisoners are presumed to be innocent and shall be treated as such.

(3) Without prejudice to legal rules for the protection of individual liberty or prescribing the procedure to be observed in respect of untried prisoners, these prisoners shall benefit by a special regime which is described in the following rules in its essential requirements only.

85.   (1) Untried prisoners shall be kept separate from convicted prisoners.

(2) Young untried prisoners shall be kept separate from adults and shall in principle be detained in separate institutions.

86. Untried prisoners shall sleep singly in separate rooms, with the reservation of different local custom in respect of the climate.

87. Within the limits compatible with the good order of the institution, untried prisoners may, if they so desire, have their food procured at their own expense from the outside, either through the administration or through their family or friends. Otherwise, the administration shall provide their food.

88.   (1) An untried prisoner shall be allowed to wear his own clothing if it is clean and suitable.

(2) If he wears prison dress, it shall be different from that supplied to convicted prisoners.

89. An untried prisoner shall always be offered opportunity to work, but shall not be required to work. If he chooses to work, he shall be paid for it.

90. An untried prisoner shall be allowed to procure at his own expense or at the expense of a third party such books, newspapers, writing materials and other means of occupation as are compatible with the interests of the administration of justice and the security and good order of the institution.

91. An untried prisoner shall be allowed to be visited and treated by his own doctor or dentist if there is reasonable ground for his application and he is able to pay any expenses incurred.

92. An untried prisoner shall be allowed to inform immediately his family of his detention and shall be given all reasonable facilities for communicating with his family and friends, and for receiving visits from them, subject only to restrictions and supervision as are necessary in the

interests of the administration of justice and of the security and good order of the institution.

93. For the purposes of his defence, an untried prisoner shall be allowed to apply for free legal aid where such aid is available, and to receive visits from his legal adviser with a view to his defence and to prepare and hand to him confidential instructions. For these purposes, he shall if he so desires be supplied with writing material. Interviews between the prisoner and his legal adviser may be within sight but not within the hearing of a police or institution official.

D. CIVIL PRISONERS

94. In countries where the law permits imprisonment for debt, or by order of a court under any other non-criminal process, persons so imprisoned shall not be subjected to any greater restriction or severity than is necessary to ensure safe custody and good order. Their treatment shall be not less favourable than that of untried prisoners, with the reservation, however, that they may possibly be required to work.

E. PERSONS ARRESTED OR DETAINED WITHOUT CHARGE

95. Without prejudice to the provisions of article 9 of the International Covenant on Civil and Political Rights, persons arrested or imprisoned without charge shall be accorded the same protection as that accorded under part I and II, section C. Relevant provisions of part II, section A, shall likewise be applicable where their application may be conducive to the benefit of this special group of persons in custody, provided that no measures shall be taken implying that re-education or rehabilitation is in any way appropriate to persons not convicted of any criminal offence.